Next.js for Modern Developers

Developers

Advanced Techniques for Building Modern and Dynamic Web Apps with Next.js

Thompson Carey

Table of Contents

Preface

Hey, fellow developer! If you're picking up this book, you're likely someone who wants to build truly impressive web applications. You're probably already comfortable with the basics of Next.js, and you're ready to take your skills to the next level. I get it! I've been there too. And that's exactly why I wrote this book. I wanted to create a resource that goes beyond the typical introductory material and provides you with the practical, advanced techniques you need to create modern, dynamic, and high-performance web experiences.

Background and Motivation

When I started working with Next.js, I was amazed by its power and flexibility. However, I quickly realized that many resources focused on the fundamentals, leaving a gap when it came to advanced topics. I spent countless hours piecing together information from various sources, experimenting, and learning from my own projects. This experience sparked a desire to create a comprehensive guide that would save you that time and effort. I wanted to share the techniques I've learned, the patterns I found most effective, and the real-world solutions that truly make a difference.

Purpose and Scope

This book is designed to equip you with the advanced knowledge and skills necessary to build robust, scalable, and performant web applications using Next.js. We'll explore complex routing, efficient data fetching, powerful API creation, state management, performance optimization, and deployment strategies. We'll also cover testing and debugging, ensuring you can deliver reliable and maintainable code. The goal is to give you a strong foundation in the advanced aspects of Next.js, empowering you to create exceptional web applications.

Target Audience

This book is written for developers who have a solid understanding of React and basic Next.js concepts. If you've built a few projects and are looking to expand your expertise, this book is for you. Whether you're a front-end developer aiming to become a full-stack engineer, or a seasoned developer looking to master Next.js, you'll find valuable information and practical guidance here.

Organization and Structure

The book is structured to guide you through a logical progression of advanced topics. We begin with a deeper look at Next.js architecture and routing, then move into data fetching and API development. We then discuss state management and advanced component patterns. The last part focuses on performance, deployment, and testing, providing you with the tools to build production-ready applications. Each chapter includes practical examples and code snippets to illustrate the concepts, and real-world scenarios to help you apply what you learn.

Invitation to Read

I'm genuinely excited for you to start reading this book. I believe you'll find it incredibly helpful in your journey to becoming a Next.js expert. I've put a lot of passion and effort into creating a resource that's both informative and approachable. Consider this book a conversation with a fellow developer, sharing insights and practical tips. So, grab a cup of coffee, open your code editor, and let's build some amazing web applications together. I hope you enjoy it!

Chapter 1: Deep Dive into Next.js Architecture

Okay, so you're ready to really understand how Next.js works under the hood, right? That's awesome, because this chapter is all about getting to the core of it. We're going to break down the key concepts that make Next.js such a powerful tool for building web applications.

1.1 Understanding Server-Side Rendering (SSR)

Alright, let's have a thorough conversation about Server-Side Rendering (SSR) in Next.js. I want you to really understand this concept, because it's foundational to building performant web applications.

So, let's start with the basics. You're probably used to how typical React applications work. When a user visits a React app, the browser downloads a minimal HTML file and a bunch of JavaScript. That JavaScript then runs in the browser to build the entire page. This is called Client-Side Rendering (CSR).

Now, with SSR, Next.js takes a different approach. Instead of the browser building the page, Next.js does that work on the server. When a user requests a page, the server executes your React code, generates the complete HTML, and sends that HTML to the browser. The browser can then immediately display the page.

Why is this a big deal? Well, there are a couple of major advantages. First, it's fantastic for Search Engine Optimization (SEO). Search engines like Google crawl your pages and index their content. With CSR, the initial HTML is often empty, so search engines have to execute JavaScript to see the content. This can be tricky and slow. With SSR, the content is already in the

HTML, making it easy for search engines to understand and index your pages.

Second, SSR improves perceived performance. Users see content faster. Imagine you visit a website and see a blank screen for a few seconds while the JavaScript loads. That's a poor user experience. With SSR, the user sees the page content almost instantly, even before the JavaScript is fully loaded. This is a huge win for user engagement.

Let's look at a practical example. Suppose you have a blog. With CSR, when a user visits a blog post, they might see a loading spinner for a few seconds. With SSR, they see the blog post content immediately, and then the page becomes interactive when the JavaScript finishes loading.

Now, how do we implement SSR in Next.js? Next.js provides a special function called getServerSideProps. This function runs on the server for every request. It allows you to fetch data and pass it as props to your page component.

Here's a basic example:

```JavaScript
// pages/blog/[id].js


function BlogPost({ post }) {

  return (

    <div>

      <h1>{post.title}</h1>

      <p>{post.content}</p>
```

```
        </div>

    );

}


export async function getServerSideProps(context)
{

    const { id } = context.params;

    const res = await
fetch(`https://api.example.com/posts/${id}`);

    const post = await res.json();


    return {

        props: {

            post,

        },

    };

}


export default BlogPost;
```

In this example, getServerSideProps fetches a blog post from an API based on the id from the URL. It then passes the post data as props to the BlogPost component.

Let's break this down:

1. context.params contains the route parameters. In this case, it's the id from [id].js.
2. We fetch data from an API using the id.
3. We return an object with a props property. This object contains the data that will be passed to the page component.

Now, let's talk about some important considerations. SSR can be slower than SSG, especially if you're fetching a lot of data. Every time a user requests a page, the server has to fetch the data and generate the HTML. This can add latency.

Here are some best practices:

- Cache data: If your data doesn't change frequently, cache it on the server to reduce the load on your API.
- Optimize API calls: Make sure your API is fast and efficient. Avoid unnecessary data fetching.
- Use CDN: A Content Delivery Network (CDN) can help deliver your HTML faster.

Here's an exercise for you. Create a page that fetches and displays a list of users from a public API using getServerSideProps.

```javascript
// pages/users.js


function Users({ users }) {

  return (

    <div>

      <h1>Users</h1>
```

```
      <ul>

        {users.map((user) => (

          <li key={user.id}>{user.name}</li>

        ))}

      </ul>

    </div>

  );

}



export async function getServerSideProps() {

  const res = await
fetch('https://jsonplaceholder.typicode.com/users
');

  const users = await res.json();


  return {

    props: {

      users,

    },

  };

}
```

```
export default Users;
```

Try to build this, and then experiment with making it more efficient. For example, you can implement a basic caching mechanism.

In real-world applications, SSR is crucial for pages that need to be indexed by search engines or for pages that require up-to-date data on every request. For example, an e-commerce product page might use SSR to display the latest product information. A news website might use SSR to display the latest articles.

Think about it like this: if you have a page that needs to be dynamic, and needs to be seen by search engines, SSR is your friend. But, if you have a page where the content rarely changes, then you'd want to use SSG.

By understanding SSR, you can build web applications that are both fast and SEO-friendly. It's a powerful tool in your Next.js arsenal.

1.2 Static Site Generation (SSG) and Incremental Static Regeneration (ISR)

Alright, let's talk about Static Site Generation (SSG) and Incremental Static Regeneration (ISR). These are powerful features in Next.js that allow you to build incredibly fast and efficient web applications. It's a real treat to work with these, and I'm excited to walk you through them.

First, let's get into Static Site Generation (SSG). With SSG, Next.js generates the HTML for your pages at build time.[1] This means that when a user requests a page, the server simply sends the pre-built

HTML. There's no need for the server to execute any JavaScript or fetch any data. This makes SSG incredibly fast.

Think of it like this: You're baking cookies. With SSG, you bake all the cookies ahead of time, and when someone wants a cookie, you just hand them one. You don't have to bake a new cookie every time someone asks.

Why would you use SSG? Well, it's perfect for content that doesn't change frequently. For example, blog posts, documentation, or marketing pages. Because the pages are generated once, they can be served from a CDN, which makes them incredibly fast.

Here's how you can implement SSG in Next.js:

JavaScript

```javascript
// pages/blog/[slug].js


function BlogPost({ post }) {

  return (

    <div>

      <h1>{post.title}</h1>

      <p>{post.content}</p>

    </div>

  );

}
```

```javascript
export async function getStaticPaths() {

  const res = await
fetch('https://api.example.com/posts');

  const posts = await res.json();


  const paths = posts.map((post) => ({

    params: { slug: post.slug },

  }));


  return {

    paths,

    fallback: false,

  };
}


export async function getStaticProps({ params })
{

  const { slug } = params;

  const res = await
fetch(`https://api.example.com/posts/${slug}`);

  const post = await res.json();
```

```
  return {

    props: {

      post,

    },

  };

}


export default BlogPost;
```

Let's break this down:

1. getStaticPaths generates the paths for all the dynamic routes. In this case, it fetches all the blog posts and creates a path for each one.
2. getStaticProps fetches the data for a specific post based on the slug from the URL. It then passes the post data as props to the BlogPost component.

fallback: false means that if a user requests a path that wasn't generated at build time, they'll see a 404 page.

Now, let's talk about Incremental Static Regeneration (ISR). This is where things get really interesting. ISR allows you to update static pages after they've been built.[2] This means you get the performance benefits of SSG with the flexibility of dynamic content.

With ISR, you can set a revalidation time. Next.js will regenerate the pages in the background at the specified intervals.[3] This allows you to keep your static pages up-to-date without rebuilding your entire site.

Here's how you can add ISR to the previous example:

```javascript
JavaScript

// pages/blog/[slug].js


// ... (BlogPost component)


export async function getStaticPaths() {

  // ... (same as before)

}



export async function getStaticProps({ params })
{

  const { slug } = params;

  const res = await
fetch(`https://api.example.com/posts/${slug}`);

  const post = await res.json();


  return {

    props: {

      post,

    },
```

```
    revalidate: 10, // Regenerate every 10
seconds

  };

}
```

```
export default BlogPost;
```

The only change is the revalidate property in getStaticProps. This tells Next.js to regenerate the page every 10 seconds.

Here's an exercise for you. Create a page that displays a list of products using SSG and ISR. The product data should be fetched from a public API. Use a revalidation time of 60 seconds.

JavaScript

```
// pages/products.js
```

```
function Products({ products }) {

  return (

    <div>

      <h1>Products</h1>

      <ul>

        {products.map((product) => (

          <li
key={product.id}>{product.title}</li>

        ))}
```

```
      </ul>

    </div>

  );

}


export async function getStaticProps() {

  const res = await
fetch('https://fakestoreapi.com/products');

  const products = await res.json();


  return {

    props: {

      products,

    },

    revalidate: 60,

  };

}


export default Products;
```

In real-world applications, SSG and ISR are used for a variety of use cases. For example, a news website might use ISR to update their articles every few minutes. An e-commerce website might use SSG for their product pages and ISR to update stock levels.[4]

When you're building a website, think about how often your content changes. If it changes rarely, use SSG. If it changes more often, use ISR. This will help you build fast and efficient web applications.

1.3 Next.js Routing and File System Conventions

Let's discuss Next.js routing, an area where Next.js really shines. It's a simple, yet powerful system that makes building complex applications feel straightforward. Next.js uses a file-system-based router, which means your routes are directly tied to the structure of your pages directory. This approach is intuitive and makes it easy to understand how your application's routes are organized.

If you create a file named about.js inside the pages directory, Next.js automatically creates a route at /about. The content of your about.js file will be rendered when a user navigates to /about. This is the most basic form of routing in Next.js.

JavaScript

```
// pages/about.js


function AboutPage() {

  return (

    <div>

      <h1>About Us</h1>
```

```
    <p>This is the about page.</p>

  </div>

 );

}
```

```
export default AboutPage;
```

Now, let's look at dynamic routes. These are routes that can accept parameters. For example, a blog post might have a URL like /posts/123, where 123 is the ID of the post. Next.js uses square brackets to denote dynamic segments in a route.

If you create a file named [id].js inside the pages/posts directory, Next.js will create a route at /posts/:id. The :id part is dynamic and can be accessed using context.params in getServerSideProps or getStaticProps.

`JavaScript`

```
// pages/posts/[id].js
```

```
function Post({ post }) {

  return (

    <div>

      <h1>{post.title}</h1>

      <p>{post.content}</p>

    </div>
```

```
  );

}


export async function getServerSideProps(context)
{

  const { id } = context.params;

  const res = await
fetch(`https://api.example.com/posts/${id}`);

  const post = await res.json();


  return {

    props: {

      post,

    },

  };

}


export default Post;
```

In this example, context.params.id contains the value of the dynamic segment.

Next.js also supports nested routes. If you create a directory structure like pages/users/profile.js, Next.js will create a route at

/users/profile. This allows you to organize your routes in a hierarchical manner.

JavaScript

```
// pages/users/profile.js
```

```
function UserProfile() {

  return (

    <div>

      <h1>User Profile</h1>

      <p>This is the user profile page.</p>

    </div>

  );

}
```

```
export default UserProfile;
```

To navigate between pages, Next.js provides the Link component. This component is an optimized version of the HTML <a> tag. It preloads pages in the background, making navigation faster.

JavaScript

```
// pages/index.js
```

```
import Link from 'next/link';
```

```
function HomePage() {

  return (

    <div>

      <h1>Welcome to the Home Page</h1>

      <Link href="/about">

        <a>Go to About Page</a>

      </Link>

      <Link href="/posts/123">

        <a>Go to Post 123</a>

      </Link>

    </div>

  );

}
```

```
export default HomePage;
```

The Link component takes a href prop, which specifies the destination URL. It also accepts an as prop, which allows you to specify a different URL to display in the browser's address bar. This is useful for SEO and user experience.

In addition to page routes, Next.js also supports API routes. These are serverless functions that allow you to create APIs within your

Next.js application. API routes are created in the pages/api directory.

JavaScript

```
// pages/api/users.js
```

```
export default function handler(req, res) {

  res.status(200).json({ name: 'John Doe' });

}
```

This creates an API endpoint at /api/users. You can use this endpoint to fetch data from your application.

Here's an exercise for you. Create a blog with dynamic routes for each blog post. Each blog post should have a title and content. Use the Link component to navigate between the posts. Also, create an API route that returns a list of all blog posts.

JavaScript

```
// pages/blog/[slug].js
```

```
function BlogPost({ post }) {

  return (

    <div>

      <h1>{post.title}</h1>

      <p>{post.content}</p>
```

```
      </div>

  );

}


export async function getServerSideProps(context)
{

  const { slug } = context.params;

  const res = await
fetch(`http://localhost:3000/api/posts/${slug}`);

  const post = await res.json();


  return {

    props: {

      post,

    },

  };

}


export default BlogPost;


// pages/index.js
```

```
import Link from 'next/link';


function HomePage({ posts }) {

  return (

    <div>

      <h1>Blog Posts</h1>

      <ul>

        {posts.map((post) => (

          <li key={post.slug}>

            <Link href={`/blog/${post.slug}`}>

              <a>{post.title}</a>

            </Link>

          </li>

        ))}

      </ul>

    </div>

  );

}
```

```
export async function getServerSideProps() {

  const res = await
fetch('http://localhost:3000/api/posts');

  const posts = await res.json();


  return {

    props: {

      posts,

    },

  };

}



export default HomePage;



// pages/api/posts.js



const posts = [

  { slug: 'post-1', title: 'Post 1', content:
'Content 1' },

  { slug: 'post-2', title: 'Post 2', content:
'Content 2' },

];
```

```
export default function handler(req, res) {

  if (req.query.slug) {

    const post = posts.find((p) => p.slug ===
req.query.slug);

    if (post) {

      res.status(200).json(post);

    } else {

      res.status(404).json({ message: 'Post not
found' });

    }

  } else {

    res.status(200).json(posts);

  }

}
```

This example shows how to use dynamic routes, the Link component, and API routes in a real-world scenario.

By understanding Next.js routing and file system conventions, you can build complex and well-organized web applications.

Chapter 2: Advanced Routing and Navigation

We've already touched on the basics of routing, but there's so much more to it. We're going to examine dynamic routes, nested routes, layout patterns, middleware, and route protection. These concepts are essential for building robust and scalable applications.

2.1 Dynamic Routes and Parameter Handling

Let's really get into the details of dynamic routes and parameter handling in Next.js. This is where you start to create applications that respond to user input and provide tailored experiences, and it's a critical skill to master.

Dynamic routes in Next.js allow you to create pages that can display different content based on parameters in the URL. For example, if you have a blog, you might want a page that displays a specific blog post based on its ID or slug. This is where dynamic routes come in handy.

To create a dynamic route, you use square brackets in the filename. For example, [id].js creates a dynamic route that matches any URL with a single segment. So, /posts/123 or /products/abc would match this route.

JavaScript

```
// pages/posts/[id].js



import { useRouter } from 'next/router';
```

```javascript
function Post() {

  const router = useRouter();

  const { id } = router.query;


  return (

    <div>

      <h1>Post {id}</h1>

      {/* Fetch and display post data here */}

    </div>

  );

}
```

```javascript
export default Post;
```

In this example, we use the useRouter hook from next/router to access the query object, which contains the dynamic parameters. The id parameter is then used to display the post ID on the page.

Now, let's talk about how to fetch data based on these dynamic parameters. If you're using getServerSideProps or getStaticProps, you can access the parameters using context.params.

JavaScript

```javascript
// pages/posts/[id].js
```

```
function Post({ post }) {

  return (

    <div>

      <h1>{post.title}</h1>

      <p>{post.content}</p>

    </div>

  );

}


export async function getServerSideProps(context)
{

  const { id } = context.params;


  // Simulate fetching data from an API
  const post = {

    id: id,

    title: `Post ${id} Title`,

    content: `Post ${id} Content`,

  };
```

```
    return {

      props: {

        post,

      },

    };

}
```

```
export default Post;
```

In this example, context.params.id contains the value of the dynamic segment. We use this value to fetch the post data and pass it as props to the Post component.

You can also create nested dynamic routes. For example, pages/products/[productId]/reviews/[reviewId].js creates a route that matches URLs like /products/123/reviews/456.

JavaScript

```
//
pages/products/[productId]/reviews/[reviewId].js


import { useRouter } from 'next/router';


function ProductReview() {

  const router = useRouter();

  const { productId, reviewId } = router.query;
```

```
    return (

      <div>

        <h1>Product {productId} Review
{reviewId}</h1>

        {/* Fetch and display review data here */}

      </div>

    );

}
```

```
export default ProductReview;
```

In this case, router.query contains both productId and reviewId.

Catch-all routes are another powerful feature. They allow you to match any number of dynamic segments. You create a catch-all route by using three dots inside the square brackets, like [...slug].js.

JavaScript

```
// pages/docs/[...slug].js
```

```
import { useRouter } from 'next/router';
```

```
function Docs() {
```

```
  const router = useRouter();

  const { slug } = router.query;


  return (

    <div>

      <h1>Docs</h1>

      <p>Slug: {slug?.join('/')}</p>

      {/* Fetch and display documentation here
*/}

    </div>

  );

}
```

```
export default Docs;
```

If you navigate to /docs/a/b/c, slug will be ['a', 'b', 'c']. This is useful for building documentation or file browsing applications.

Here's an exercise: Create a dynamic route that displays a product and all its reviews. Use nested dynamic routes to achieve this.

JavaScript

```
// pages/products/[productId].js
```

```
import { useRouter } from 'next/router';
```

```jsx
import Link from 'next/link';


function Product() {

  const router = useRouter();

  const { productId } = router.query;


  return (

    <div>

      <h1>Product {productId}</h1>

      <Link
href={`/products/${productId}/reviews/1`}>

        <a>Review 1</a>

      </Link>

      <Link
href={`/products/${productId}/reviews/2`}>

        <a>Review 2</a>

      </Link>

    </div>

  );

}
```

```
export default Product;


// pages/products/[productId]/reviews/[reviewId].js


import { useRouter } from 'next/router';


function ProductReview() {

  const router = useRouter();

  const { productId, reviewId } = router.query;


  return (

    <div>

      <h1>Product {productId} Review
{reviewId}</h1>

      {/* Fetch and display review data here */}

    </div>

  );

}


export default ProductReview;
```

In real-world applications, dynamic routes are used extensively. For example, an e-commerce website might use dynamic routes to display product pages, category pages, and search results. A social media platform might use dynamic routes to display user profiles, posts, and comments.

By understanding dynamic routes and parameter handling, you can build applications that are flexible, scalable, and provide a great user experience. It's a fundamental concept that you'll use in almost every Next.js project.

2.2 Nested Routes and Layout Patterns

Let's delve into nested routes and layout patterns, a powerful combination that allows you to create complex, organized, and maintainable applications. This is where you really start to see the organizational power of Next.js, and how it helps you manage your application's structure.

Nested routes, as the name suggests, allow you to create routes within routes. This mirrors how you might organize a complex web application with distinct sections. For instance, you might have a dashboard with multiple sub-sections like /dashboard/profile, /dashboard/settings, and /dashboard/reports.

In Next.js, you achieve this by creating a folder structure within the pages directory. So, to create the dashboard routes mentioned above, you would create a dashboard folder inside pages, and then place profile.js, settings.js, and reports.js inside the dashboard folder.

```
JavaScript

// pages/dashboard/profile.js
```

```
function Profile() {

  return (

    <div>

      <h1>User Profile</h1>

      {/* Profile content here */}

    </div>

  );

}


export default Profile;


// pages/dashboard/settings.js


function Settings() {

  return (

    <div>

      <h1>User Settings</h1>

      {/* Settings content here */}

    </div>

  );
```

```
}


export default Settings;


// pages/dashboard/reports.js


function Reports() {

  return (

    <div>

      <h1>User Reports</h1>

      {/* Reports content here */}

    </div>

  );

}


export default Reports;
```

This folder structure automatically translates to the URL structure, and Next.js handles the routing for you.

Now, let's talk about layout patterns. This is where you can create reusable UI components that wrap your pages. For example, you might have a common layout for all dashboard pages, with a sidebar and header.

One way to achieve this is by creating a layout component and wrapping your pages with it.

JavaScript

```
// components/DashboardLayout.js


function DashboardLayout({ children }) {

  return (

    <div>

      <nav>

        {/* Dashboard navigation here */}

      </nav>

      <main>{children}</main>

    </div>

  );

}


export default DashboardLayout;
```

Then, in your pages, you can import and use this layout component.

JavaScript

```
// pages/dashboard/profile.js
```

```
import DashboardLayout from
'../../components/DashboardLayout';


function Profile() {

  return (

    <div>

      <h1>User Profile</h1>

      {/* Profile content here */}

    </div>

  );

}



Profile.getLayout = function getLayout(page) {

  return
<DashboardLayout>{page}</DashboardLayout>;

};



export default Profile;
```

Notice the getLayout function. This is a Next.js convention that allows you to specify a layout for a page. The page argument is the page component itself, and you can wrap it with your layout component.

This pattern is incredibly powerful because it allows you to create consistent layouts across your application. You can have different layouts for different sections, such as an admin layout, a user layout, and a public layout.

Here's a more complex example. Imagine you have an e-commerce application. You might have a layout for the product pages, with a sidebar for filtering and a header for navigation.

```javascript
// components/ProductLayout.js


function ProductLayout({ children }) {

  return (

    <div>

      <header>

        {/* Navigation here */}

      </header>

      <aside>

        {/* Filtering sidebar here */}

      </aside>

      <main>{children}</main>

      <footer>

        {/* Footer here */}

      </footer>
```

```
      </div>

    );

}


export default ProductLayout;


// pages/products/[id].js


import ProductLayout from
'../../components/ProductLayout';


function ProductPage() {

  return (

    <div>

      {/* Product details here */}

    </div>

  );

}


ProductPage.getLayout = function getLayout(page)
{
```

```javascript
  return <ProductLayout>{page}</ProductLayout>;

};
```

```javascript
export default ProductPage;
```

This approach not only keeps your code organized but also makes it easier to maintain and update.

Here's an exercise for you: Create an admin dashboard with nested routes for users, products, and orders. Use a layout component to provide a consistent layout for all admin pages.

JavaScript

```javascript
// components/AdminLayout.js


function AdminLayout({ children }) {

  return (

    <div>

      <nav>

        {/* Admin navigation here */}

      </nav>

      <main>{children}</main>

    </div>

  );

}
```

```
export default AdminLayout;


// pages/admin/users.js


import AdminLayout from
'../../components/AdminLayout';


function Users() {

  return (

    <div>

      <h1>Admin Users</h1>

      {/* Users content here */}

    </div>

  );

}


Users.getLayout = function getLayout(page) {

  return <AdminLayout>{page}</AdminLayout>;

};
```

```
export default Users;


// pages/admin/products.js


import AdminLayout from
'../../components/AdminLayout';


function Products() {

  return (

    <div>

      <h1>Admin Products</h1>

      {/* Products content here */}

    </div>

  );

}


Products.getLayout = function getLayout(page) {

  return <AdminLayout>{page}</AdminLayout>;

};


export default Products;
```

```javascript
// pages/admin/orders.js

import AdminLayout from
'../../components/AdminLayout';

function Orders() {

  return (

    <div>

      <h1>Admin Orders</h1>

      {/* Orders content here */}

    </div>

  );

}


Orders.getLayout = function getLayout(page) {

  return <AdminLayout>{page}</AdminLayout>;

};


export default Orders;
```

This exercise will give you practical experience in using nested routes and layout patterns.

By mastering nested routes and layout patterns, you can build complex applications that are easy to navigate, maintain, and scale. It's a key skill for any Next.js developer.

2.3 Middleware and Route Protection

Let's discuss middleware and route protection in Next.js. This is where you start to control the flow of your application, ensuring that only authorized users can access certain parts and that your application behaves as expected. It's a critical aspect of building secure and robust web applications.

Middleware in Next.js allows you to run code before a request is completed.[1] This is incredibly powerful for tasks like authentication, authorization, logging, and more.[2] Think of it as a gatekeeper that intercepts requests and decides what to do with them.

You create middleware by placing a middleware.js or middleware.ts file in the pages directory or the root of your project. Next.js will automatically run this code for every request.[3]

Here's a basic example of using middleware for authentication:

```
JavaScript

// middleware.js


import { NextResponse } from 'next/server';
```

```
export function middleware(req) {

  const token = req.cookies.get('token');


  if (!token &&
req.nextUrl.pathname.startsWith('/dashboard')) {

    return NextResponse.redirect(new
URL('/login', req.url));

  }



  return NextResponse.next();

}
```

In this example, the middleware checks for a token cookie. If the token is missing and the user is trying to access a page under /dashboard, they are redirected to the login page. Otherwise, the request is allowed to proceed.

Let's break this down:

- req.cookies.get('token') retrieves the token cookie from the request.
- req.nextUrl.pathname gets the pathname of the requested URL.
- NextResponse.redirect(new URL('/login', req.url)) redirects the user to the login page.
- NextResponse.next() allows the request to proceed to the next handler.

You can also use middleware to modify the request or response.[4] For example, you can add headers, rewrite URLs, or set cookies.[5]

```
JavaScript

// middleware.js


import { NextResponse } from 'next/server';


export function middleware(req) {

  const response = NextResponse.next();

  response.headers.set('X-Custom-Header', 'Hello
from middleware');

  return response;

}
```

In this example, we add a custom header to the response.

Now, let's talk about route protection. This is closely related to middleware and involves protecting certain routes from unauthorized access. You can achieve this using middleware or by checking authentication status in getServerSideProps.

Here's an example of using getServerSideProps for route protection:

```
JavaScript

// pages/dashboard/profile.js


import { getSession } from 'next-auth/react';
```

```
function Profile() {

  return (

    <div>

      <h1>User Profile</h1>

      {/* Profile content here */}

    </div>

  );

}


export async function getServerSideProps(context)
{

  const session = await getSession(context);


  if (!session) {

    return {

      redirect: {

        destination: '/login',

        permanent: false,

      },

    };
```

```
  }



  return {

    props: {},

  };

}
```

```
export default Profile;
```

In this example, we use getSession from next-auth/react to check if the user is authenticated. If they are not, they are redirected to the login page.

Here's a more complex example using middleware to protect multiple routes:

JavaScript

```
// middleware.js
```

```
import { NextResponse } from 'next/server';

import { getSession } from 'next-auth/react';


export async function middleware(req) {

  const session = await getSession({ req });
```

```javascript
  if (!session &&
req.nextUrl.pathname.startsWith('/dashboard')) {

    return NextResponse.redirect(new
URL('/login', req.url));

  }



  return NextResponse.next();

}
```

This middleware uses next-auth/react to check for a session and protects all routes under /dashboard.

Here's an exercise for you: Create a middleware that logs the user's IP address for every request. Also, create a protected route that requires authentication. Use next-auth/react to handle authentication.

JavaScript

```javascript
// middleware.js


import { NextResponse } from 'next/server';

import { getSession } from 'next-auth/react';


export async function middleware(req) {

  console.log(`User IP: ${req.ip}`);
```

```
    const session = await getSession({ req });


    if (!session &&
req.nextUrl.pathname.startsWith('/admin')) {

       return NextResponse.redirect(new
URL('/login', req.url));

    }


    return NextResponse.next();

}


// pages/admin/dashboard.js


import { getSession } from 'next-auth/react';


function AdminDashboard() {
    return (
      <div>
        <h1>Admin Dashboard</h1>
      </div>
    );
```

```
}


export async function getServerSideProps(context)
{

  const session = await getSession(context);


  if (!session) {

    return {

      redirect: {

        destination: '/login',

        permanent: false,

      },

    };

  }


  return {

    props: {},

  };

}


export default AdminDashboard;
```

This exercise will give you practical experience in using middleware and route protection.

By mastering middleware and route protection, you can build secure and robust web applications that provide a great user experience. It's a key skill for any Next.js developer.

Chapter 3: Data Fetching Mastery

Data fetching is a core part of any web application. Next.js provides powerful tools for fetching data on the server and client sides, allowing you to build dynamic and performant applications. Let's dig into each of these methods and see how they can be used effectively.

3.1 getServerSideProps and getStaticProps Deep Dive

Okay, let's really get into the heart of server-side data fetching with getServerSideProps and getStaticProps. These are crucial tools in Next.js for building high-performance, dynamic applications. Understanding how they work, and when to use each, is essential for any serious Next.js developer.

Let's start with getServerSideProps. This function runs on the server for every request to the page. It's designed for situations where you need to fetch data that changes frequently, or data that's specific to the user making the request.

Think of it this way: You have a dashboard that displays the user's latest activity. Every time the user visits the dashboard, you need to fetch their activity from the database. This is a perfect use case for getServerSideProps.

Here's a basic example:

```javascript
// pages/dashboard.js


function Dashboard({ activity }) {
```

```
  return (

    <div>

      <h1>Latest Activity</h1>

      <ul>

        {activity.map((item) => (

          <li
key={item.id}>{item.description}</li>

        ))}

      </ul>

    </div>

  );

}


export async function getServerSideProps(context)
{

  // Simulate fetching user's activity from a
database

  const activity = [

    { id: 1, description: 'Logged in' },

    { id: 2, description: 'Posted a comment' },

    { id: 3, description: 'Updated profile' },

  ];
```

```
  return {

    props: {

      activity,

    },

  };

}
```

```
export default Dashboard;
```

In this example, getServerSideProps simulates fetching the user's activity and passes it as props to the Dashboard component. The key thing to remember is that this function runs on the server for every request.

Now, let's talk about getStaticProps. This function runs at build time. It's used for fetching data that doesn't change frequently, or data that can be pre-rendered at build time.

Think of it like this: You have a blog. The blog posts are written once and rarely change. This is a perfect use case for getStaticProps.

Here's an example:

```
JavaScript
```

```
// pages/blog/[slug].js
```

```
function BlogPost({ post }) {

  return (

    <div>

      <h1>{post.title}</h1>

      <p>{post.content}</p>

    </div>

  );

}



export async function getStaticProps({ params })
{

  const { slug } = params;


  // Simulate fetching a blog post from a
database

  const posts = [

    { slug: 'post-1', title: 'Post 1 Title',
content: 'Post 1 Content' },

    { slug: 'post-2', title: 'Post 2 Title',
content: 'Post 2 Content' },

  ];
```

```
  const post = posts.find((p) => p.slug ===
slug);


  return {

    props: {

      post,

    },

  };

}


export async function getStaticPaths() {

  const posts = [

    { slug: 'post-1' },

    { slug: 'post-2' },

  ];


  const paths = posts.map((post) => ({

    params: { slug: post.slug },

  }));


  return {
```

```
    paths,

    fallback: false,

  };

}
```

```
export default BlogPost;
```

In this example, getStaticProps fetches a blog post based on the slug from the URL. getStaticPaths generates the paths for all the blog posts. The important thing to note is that this function runs at build time.

Now, let's talk about the key differences and when to use each.

getServerSideProps:

- Runs on every request.
- Ideal for dynamic data that changes frequently.
- Can be slower than getStaticProps because it runs on every request.
- Good for user specific data.

getStaticProps:

- Runs at build time.
- Ideal for static data that doesn't change frequently.
- Incredibly fast because the data is pre-rendered.
- Good for SEO.

Let's look at some real-world examples:

- An e-commerce product page: If the product data changes frequently (e.g., stock levels), you might use getServerSideProps. If the product data is relatively static, you might use getStaticProps.
- A news website: If you need to display the latest news articles, you might use getServerSideProps. If you're displaying archived articles, you might use getStaticProps.
- A user dashboard: getServerSideProps is the best option, because you want the most up to date information.

Here's an exercise for you: Create a page that displays a list of users. The user data should be fetched from a public API. Use getServerSideProps to fetch the data. Then, create a page that displays a list of blog posts. The blog post data should be fetched from a local JSON file. Use getStaticProps to fetch the data.

JavaScript

```javascript
// pages/users.js


function Users({ users }) {

  return (

    <div>

      <h1>Users</h1>

      <ul>

        {users.map((user) => (

          <li key={user.id}>{user.name}</li>

        ))}
```

```
      </ul>

    </div>

  );

}


export async function getServerSideProps() {

  const res = await
fetch('https://jsonplaceholder.typicode.com/users
');

  const users = await res.json();


  return {

    props: {

      users,

    },

  };

}


export default Users;


// pages/blog.js
```

```
function Blog({ posts }) {

  return (

    <div>

      <h1>Blog Posts</h1>

      <ul>

        {posts.map((post) => (

          <li key={post.id}>{post.title}</li>

        ))}

      </ul>

    </div>

  );

}


export async function getStaticProps() {

  const posts = [

    { id: 1, title: 'Post 1' },

    { id: 2, title: 'Post 2' },

  ];
```

```
  return {

    props: {

      posts,

    },

  };

}
```

```
export default Blog;
```

This exercise will give you practical experience in using getServerSideProps and getStaticProps.

By mastering getServerSideProps and getStaticProps, you can build Next.js applications that are both fast and dynamic. It's a fundamental skill for any Next.js developer.

3.2 getStaticPaths for Dynamic Static Generation

Let's really dig into getStaticPaths. This is a crucial function when you're working with dynamic routes and static site generation (SSG). It allows you to tell Next.js which paths should be pre-rendered at build time. It's the key to creating static pages that are based on dynamic data, and it's something you'll use a lot when building data-driven static sites.

When you use getStaticProps with dynamic routes, Next.js needs to know which versions of the page to generate at build time. That's where getStaticPaths comes in. It defines an array of paths that Next.js should pre-render.

Here's a simple example. Let's say you have a blog with posts that are identified by a slug, like /blog/my-first-post. You want to generate static pages for each blog post at build time.

JavaScript

```javascript
// pages/blog/[slug].js


function BlogPost({ post }) {

  return (

    <div>

      <h1>{post.title}</h1>

      <p>{post.content}</p>

    </div>

  );

}


export async function getStaticPaths() {

  // Simulate fetching all blog posts from a
database or API

  const posts = [

    { slug: 'my-first-post', title: 'My First
Post', content: 'Content of my first post' },

    { slug: 'my-second-post', title: 'My Second
Post', content: 'Content of my second post' },
```

```
  { slug: 'my-third-post', title: 'My Third
Post', content: 'Content of my third post' },

  ];


  const paths = posts.map((post) => ({

    params: { slug: post.slug },

  }));


  return {

    paths,

    fallback: false,

  };

}



export async function getStaticProps({ params })
{

  const { slug } = params;


  // Simulate fetching the specific blog post
based on the slug

  const posts = [
```

```
    { slug: 'my-first-post', title: 'My First
Post', content: 'Content of my first post' },

    { slug: 'my-second-post', title: 'My Second
Post', content: 'Content of my second post' },

    { slug: 'my-third-post', title: 'My Third
Post', content: 'Content of my third post' },

  ];


  const post = posts.find((p) => p.slug ===
slug);


  return {

    props: {

      post,

    },

  };

}


export default BlogPost;
```

Let's break down getStaticPaths:

- It's an async function.
- It returns an object with paths and fallback properties.

- The paths property is an array of objects, where each object defines a params property that contains the dynamic route parameters.
- The fallback property tells Next.js how to handle paths that weren't generated at build time.

In this example, we simulate fetching blog posts from a database or API. We then map over the posts and create an array of paths. Each path object contains the slug parameter, which corresponds to the [slug].js filename.

The fallback: false property tells Next.js that if a user requests a path that wasn't generated at build time, they should see a 404 page.

Now, let's talk about the fallback property in more detail.

It can have three values:

- false: If a user requests a path that wasn't generated at build time, they'll see a 404 page.
- true: If a user requests a path that wasn't generated at build time, Next.js will serve a fallback page while the page is being generated in the background. Once the page is generated, Next.js will serve the generated page.
- 'blocking': If a user requests a path that wasn't generated at build time, Next.js will block the page until the page is generated.

fallback: true is useful for cases where you have a large number of dynamic pages, and you don't want to generate them all at build time. You can generate the most popular pages at build time and then generate the rest on demand.

fallback: 'blocking' is similar to fallback: true, but it blocks the page until it's generated. This is useful for cases where you want to ensure that the user sees the fully generated page.

Here's an exercise for you: Create a page that displays a list of products from an API. Use getStaticPaths to generate static pages for each product. Use fallback: true to handle products that weren't generated at build time.

JavaScript

```javascript
// pages/products/[id].js


function Product({ product }) {

  return (

    <div>

      <h1>{product.title}</h1>

      <p>{product.description}</p>

    </div>

  );

}



export async function getStaticPaths() {

  const res = await
fetch('https://fakestoreapi.com/products');

  const products = await res.json();


  const paths = products.map((product) => ({
```

```
      params: { id: product.id.toString() },

   }));


   return {

     paths,

     fallback: true,

   };

}



export async function getStaticProps({ params })
{

   const { id } = params;

   const res = await
fetch(`https://fakestoreapi.com/products/${id}`);

   const product = await res.json();


   return {

     props: {

       product,

     },

     revalidate: 60,
```

```
    };

}
```

```
export default Product;
```

In this exercise, we fetch a list of products from the Fake Store API and generate static pages for each product. We use fallback: true to handle products that weren't generated at build time. We also use revalidate: 60 to regenerate the pages every 60 seconds.

By mastering getStaticPaths, you can build high-performance static sites that are based on dynamic data. It's a key skill for any Next.js developer.

3.3 Client-Side Data Fetching and Caching

Let's talk about client-side data fetching and caching. While Next.js excels at server-side rendering and static site generation, there are situations where you need to fetch data on the client side. This is particularly true for interactive parts of your application, or for data that changes too frequently to be pre-rendered.

Client-side data fetching means that the data is fetched and rendered in the user's browser, after the initial HTML has been loaded.[1] This approach is common in Single Page Applications (SPAs) and can be very effective for creating dynamic user experiences.[2]

The most common way to fetch data on the client side in Next.js is using the useEffect hook. This hook allows you to perform side effects in functional components, such as fetching data from an API.[3]

Here's a basic example:

JavaScript

```
// pages/posts.js

import { useState, useEffect } from 'react';

function Posts() {
  const [posts, setPosts] = useState([]);

  useEffect(() => {

fetch('https://jsonplaceholder.typicode.com/posts')

      .then((res) => res.json())

      .then((data) => setPosts(data));
  }, []);

  if (!posts.length) {
    return <div>Loading...</div>;
  }
```

```
  return (

    <div>

      <h1>Posts</h1>

      <ul>

        {posts.map((post) => (

          <li key={post.id}>{post.title}</li>

        ))}

      </ul>

    </div>

  );

}



export default Posts;
```

In this example, we use useEffect to fetch a list of posts from the JSONPlaceholder API. We then store the posts in the posts state and render them in a list.

Let's break this down:

- useState([]) initializes the posts state as an empty array.
- useEffect(() => { ... }, []) runs the effect only once, after the initial render, because the dependency array is empty.
- fetch('https://jsonplaceholder.typicode.com/posts') fetches the data from the API.
- .then((res) => res.json()) parses the response as JSON.

- .then((data) => setPosts(data)) updates the posts state with the fetched data.

Now, let's talk about caching. Caching is a technique that stores data in a temporary location, so it can be retrieved more quickly in the future.[4] This is crucial for improving the performance of your application.

There are several ways to implement caching on the client side:

- localStorage: This allows you to store data in the user's browser persistently.[5] The data is stored as key-value pairs and remains available even after the browser is closed.
- sessionStorage: This is similar to localStorage, but the data is only available for the duration of the current session. When the user closes the browser tab, the data is cleared.
- In-memory caching: This involves storing data in a JavaScript variable. The data is only available for the duration of the current page load.

Here's an example of using localStorage for caching:

JavaScript

```
// pages/posts.js



import { useState, useEffect } from 'react';



function Posts() {

  const [posts, setPosts] = useState([]);
```

```javascript
useEffect(() => {

    const cachedPosts =
localStorage.getItem('posts');


    if (cachedPosts) {

      setPosts(JSON.parse(cachedPosts));

    } else {

fetch('https://jsonplaceholder.typicode.com/posts
')

        .then((res) => res.json())

        .then((data) => {

          setPosts(data);

          localStorage.setItem('posts',
JSON.stringify(data));

        });

    }

}, []);


  if (!posts.length) {

    return <div>Loading...</div>;

  }
```

```
    return (

      <div>

        <h1>Posts</h1>

        <ul>

          {posts.map((post) => (

            <li key={post.id}>{post.title}</li>

          ))}

        </ul>

      </div>

    );

  }
```

```
export default Posts;
```

In this example, we check if the posts data is already stored in localStorage. If it is, we use the cached data. Otherwise, we fetch the data from the API and store it in localStorage.

Here's an exercise for you: Create a page that displays a list of users from an API. Use client-side data fetching to fetch the data. Implement caching using sessionStorage.

```
JavaScript
```

```
// pages/users.js
```

```javascript
import { useState, useEffect } from 'react';

function Users() {
  const [users, setUsers] = useState([]);

  useEffect(() => {

    const cachedUsers =
sessionStorage.getItem('users');

    if (cachedUsers) {

      setUsers(JSON.parse(cachedUsers));

    } else {

fetch('https://jsonplaceholder.typicode.com/users
')

        .then((res) => res.json())

        .then((data) => {

          setUsers(data);

          sessionStorage.setItem('users',
JSON.stringify(data));

        });
```

```
    }
  }, []);


  if (!users.length) {
    return <div>Loading...</div>;
  }


  return (
    <div>
      <h1>Users</h1>
      <ul>
        {users.map((user) => (
          <li key={user.id}>{user.name}</li>
        ))}
      </ul>
    </div>
  );
}


export default Users;
```

This exercise will give you practical experience in using client-side data fetching and caching.

By understanding client-side data fetching and caching, you can build dynamic and performant Next.js applications that provide a great user experience. It's an essential skill for any Next.js developer.

Chapter 4: Advanced API Routes and Serverless Functions

Next.js isn't just for building front-end applications. It also provides powerful tools for creating back-end APIs, enabling you to build full-stack applications with a single framework. Let's get into the details of creating efficient and scalable API routes, and how Next.js handles serverless and edge functions.

4.1 Building Scalable API Routes

Let's really dig into building scalable API routes in Next.js. This is a topic that's crucial as your application grows and needs to handle more complex interactions and data. You'll find that Next.js offers a straightforward way to create API endpoints right alongside your front-end code, and this can be a powerful tool in your development arsenal.

When you start building API routes in Next.js, you're essentially creating serverless functions that run on demand. This means you don't have to worry about managing servers or scaling infrastructure. Next.js handles all of that for you.

The foundation of an API route is the handler function. This function receives two arguments: req (request) and res (response). The req object contains information about the incoming request, such as the HTTP method, headers, and body. The res object allows you to send a response to the client.

Here's a basic example of creating an API route that returns a list of products:

```
JavaScript
```

```
// pages/api/products.js
```

```javascript
export default function handler(req, res) {

  const products = [

    { id: 1, name: 'Laptop', price: 1200 },

    { id: 2, name: 'Smartphone', price: 800 },

    { id: 3, name: 'Tablet', price: 500 },

  ];


  res.status(200).json(products);

}
```

In this example, when a client makes a GET request to /api/products, the handler function is executed, and it returns a JSON response containing a list of products.

However, building scalable API routes involves more than just returning static data. You need to handle different HTTP methods, validate input data, use environment variables, and implement proper error handling.

Let's look at a more complex example that demonstrates these best practices:

JavaScript

```javascript
// pages/api/orders.js


export default function handler(req, res) {
```

```javascript
if (req.method === 'GET') {

  // Handle GET request to retrieve orders

  // Simulate fetching orders from a database

  const orders = [

      { id: 1, customer: 'John Doe', items:
['Laptop'], total: 1200 },

      { id: 2, customer: 'Jane Smith', items:
['Smartphone'], total: 800 },

  ];

  res.status(200).json(orders);

} else if (req.method === 'POST') {

  // Handle POST request to create a new order

  const { customer, items, total } = req.body;


  // Validate input data

  if (!customer || !items || !total) {

    res.status(400).json({ message: 'Missing
required fields' });

    return;

  }


  // Simulate saving the order to a database
```

```
    const newOrder = { id: Date.now(), customer,
items, total };

    res.status(201).json(newOrder);

  } else {

    // Handle other HTTP methods

    res.setHeader('Allow', ['GET', 'POST']);

    res.status(405).end(`Method ${req.method} Not
Allowed`);

  }

}
```

In this example, we handle both GET and POST requests. For POST requests, we validate the input data and return an error response if any required fields are missing. We also set the Allow header to indicate which HTTP methods are supported.

Using environment variables is crucial for storing sensitive data, such as API keys and database credentials. Next.js allows you to access environment variables using the process.env object.

Here's an example of using an environment variable to store an API key:

JavaScript

```
// pages/api/weather.js


export default async function handler(req, res) {

  const apiKey = process.env.WEATHER_API_KEY;
```

```
  const { city } = req.query;



 if (!city) {

   res.status(400).json({ message: 'City is
required' });

   return;

 }



 try {

   const response = await
fetch(`https://api.openweathermap.org/data/2.5/we
ather?q=${city}&appid=${apiKey}`);

   const data = await response.json();

   res.status(200).json(data);

 } catch (error) {

   res.status(500).json({ message: 'Failed to
fetch weather data' });

 }

}
```

In this example, we fetch weather data from the OpenWeatherMap API. We use the process.env.WEATHER_API_KEY to access the API key, which should be stored in your .env.local file.

Implementing proper error handling is essential for building robust API routes. You should handle errors gracefully and return informative error responses to the client.

Here's an exercise for you: Create an API route that handles user registration. The route should accept a POST request with the user's name, email, and password. Validate the input data and return an appropriate response. Use environment variables to store any sensitive data.

JavaScript

```javascript
// pages/api/register.js


export default function handler(req, res) {

  if (req.method === 'POST') {

    const { name, email, password } = req.body;


    if (!name || !email || !password) {

      res.status(400).json({ message: 'Missing required fields' });

      return;

    }


    // Simulate saving the user to a database

    const newUser = { id: Date.now(), name, email, password };
```

```
    res.status(201).json(newUser);

  } else {

    res.setHeader('Allow', ['POST']);

    res.status(405).end(`Method ${req.method} Not
Allowed`);

  }

}
```

This exercise will give you practical experience in building scalable API routes with input validation and error handling.

By mastering these techniques, you can build robust and scalable API routes that can handle complex data interactions and provide a great user experience.

4.2 Serverless Function Implementation

Let's really get into serverless function implementation within Next.js. This is a powerful concept that allows you to build back-end logic without managing servers. It's about writing code that responds to events, and Next.js makes this remarkably approachable.

When you create API routes in Next.js, you're essentially building serverless functions. These functions are triggered by HTTP requests, and Next.js handles the scaling and execution for you. This means you can focus on writing your application's logic, without concerning yourself with server management.

The core of a serverless function in Next.js is the handler function. This function receives two arguments: req (request) and res (response). The req object contains information about the incoming request, such as the HTTP method, headers, and body. The res object allows you to send a response to the client.

Here's a simple example of a serverless function that returns a greeting:

JavaScript

```
// pages/api/hello.js
```

```
export default function handler(req, res) {

  res.status(200).json({ message: 'Hello from
Next.js serverless function!' });

}
```

In this example, when a client makes a GET request to /api/hello, the handler function is executed, and it returns a JSON response with a greeting message.

Serverless functions are ideal for a variety of tasks, such as:

- Handling form submissions
- Processing payments
- Sending emails
- Fetching data from external APIs
- Performing background tasks

Let's explore some real-world examples.

Imagine you have a contact form on your website. When a user submits the form, you want to send an email notification.

You can create a serverless function to handle this task:

JavaScript

```javascript
// pages/api/contact.js


export default async function handler(req, res) {

  if (req.method === 'POST') {

    const { name, email, message } = req.body;



    // Simulate sending an email

    try {

      // Replace with your email sending logic

      console.log(`Sending email to ${email} from ${name} with message: ${message}`);

      res.status(200).json({ message: 'Email sent successfully!' });

    } catch (error) {

      console.error('Failed to send email:', error);

      res.status(500).json({ message: 'Failed to send email' });

    }

  } else {
```

```
    res.setHeader('Allow', ['POST']);

    res.status(405).end(`Method ${req.method} Not
Allowed`);

  }

}
```

In this example, we handle POST requests to /api/contact. We
simulate sending an email using console.log, but in a real-world
application, you would replace this with your email sending logic,
such as using Nodemailer or SendGrid.

Another common use case for serverless functions is fetching data
from external APIs.

**For example, you might want to fetch weather data based
on the user's location:**

JavaScript

```
// pages/api/weather.js


export default async function handler(req, res) {

  const { city } = req.query;


  if (!city) {

    res.status(400).json({ message: 'City is
required' });

    return;
```

```
  }


  const apiKey = process.env.WEATHER_API_KEY;

  const url =
`https://api.openweathermap.org/data/2.5/weather?
q=${city}&appid=${apiKey}`;


  try {

    const response = await fetch(url);

    const data = await response.json();

    res.status(200).json(data);

  } catch (error) {

    res.status(500).json({ message: 'Failed to
fetch weather data' });

  }

}
```

In this example, we fetch weather data from the OpenWeatherMap API using the fetch function. We use the process.env object to access the API key, which should be stored in your .env.local file.

Implementing error handling is crucial for building robust serverless functions. You should handle errors gracefully and return informative error responses to the client.

Here's an exercise for you: Create a serverless function that handles user authentication. The function should accept a POST request with the user's email and password. Simulate authenticating the user and return a JSON response with a success or error message.

JavaScript

```javascript
// pages/api/login.js


export default function handler(req, res) {

  if (req.method === 'POST') {

    const { email, password } = req.body;


    // Simulate user authentication

    if (email === 'test@example.com' && password === 'password') {

      res.status(200).json({ message: 'Login successful!' });

    } else {

      res.status(401).json({ message: 'Invalid credentials' });

    }

  } else {

    res.setHeader('Allow', ['POST']);

    res.status(405).end(`Method ${req.method} Not Allowed`);
```

```
    }

}
```

This exercise will give you practical experience in building serverless functions that handle user authentication.

By understanding how to implement serverless functions in Next.js, you can build powerful and scalable backends without managing servers. It's a key skill for any Next.js developer.

4.3 Edge Functions

Okay, let's talk about edge functions in Next.js. This is a more advanced topic, but it unlocks some really powerful capabilities for optimizing your application's performance and user experience. It's about bringing your code closer to the user, and it can make a significant difference in how responsive your application feels.

Edge functions are serverless functions that run on edge servers. These servers are distributed globally, which means they're physically closer to your users than traditional servers. This reduces latency, the time it takes for data to travel between the user's device and the server, resulting in faster response times and a better user experience.

Think of it like this: Instead of having one central kitchen that serves an entire city, you have smaller kitchens located in different neighborhoods. This allows people to get their food faster because it doesn't have to travel as far. Edge functions work in a similar way.

Next.js leverages the Vercel Edge Runtime to support edge functions. This runtime is designed to be lightweight and fast, making it ideal for running code on the edge.

So, what can you do with edge functions?

Here are some common use cases:

- A/B testing: You can use edge functions to split traffic between different versions of your application and measure their performance.
- Personalization: You can personalize content based on the user's location, device, or other factors.
- Authentication: You can use edge functions to authenticate users and protect routes.
- Bot detection: You can use edge functions to detect and block bots from accessing your application.
- Redirects and rewrites: You can use edge functions to redirect or rewrite URLs based on certain conditions.

Let's start with a simple example of using an edge function to rewrite URLs:

```javascript
JavaScript

// middleware.js


import { NextResponse } from 'next/server';


export function middleware(req) {

  if
(req.nextUrl.pathname.startsWith('/old-page')) {

    return NextResponse.rewrite(new
URL('/new-page', req.url));

  }
```

```
  return NextResponse.next();

}


export const config = {

  matcher: '/old-page',

};
```

In this example, we're using middleware to rewrite any requests to /old-page to /new-page. This can be useful for migrating old URLs to new ones without breaking existing links.

Here's how it works:

- middleware.js is a special file that defines your middleware.
- The middleware function is executed for each request.
- req.nextUrl.pathname gives you the requested URL's path.
- NextResponse.rewrite() changes the URL the user sees.
- NextResponse.next() lets the request continue normally.
- config.matcher tells Next.js which paths this middleware applies to.

Now, let's look at a more complex example of using an edge function to personalize content based on the user's location.

```
JavaScript

// middleware.js


import { NextResponse } from 'next/server';

import { geoIP } from '@vercel/edge';
```

```
export async function middleware(req) {

  const { city } = geoIP.lookup(req);

  const country = geoIP.country(req);


  const response = NextResponse.next();


  if (city) {

    response.headers.set('X-User-City', city);

  }


  if (country) {

    response.headers.set('X-User-Country',
country.code);

  }


  return response;

}


export const config = {

  matcher: '/(.*)',
```

```
};
```

In this example, we're using the @vercel/edge package to get the user's city and country based on their IP address. We then set custom headers on the response with this information. This information can then be used by the application to display personalized content.

Important points to note:

- Edge functions have limitations. They are designed to be lightweight and fast, so they have restrictions on things like file system access and the amount of computation they can perform.
- You'll need a platform that supports edge functions, such as Vercel, to deploy them.
- Edge functions are a powerful tool, but they should be used judiciously. For complex operations that require a lot of computation or database access, traditional serverless functions may be more appropriate.

Here's a practical exercise for you: Create an edge function that redirects users based on their country. For example, redirect users from the UK to /uk and users from the US to /us.

```JavaScript
// middleware.js


import { NextResponse } from 'next/server';

import { geoIP } from '@vercel/edge';


export function middleware(req) {
```

```
  const country = geoIP.country(req);


  if (country?.code === 'GB') {

    return NextResponse.redirect(new URL('/uk',
req.url));

  }


  if (country?.code === 'US') {

    return NextResponse.redirect(new URL('/us',
req.url));

  }


  return NextResponse.next();

}


export const config = {

  matcher: '/(.*)',

};
```

This exercise provides hands-on experience with edge functions and geolocation.

By understanding edge functions, you can significantly enhance the performance and user experience of your Next.js applications.

They're a valuable tool for building modern, high-performance web applications.

Chapter 5: State Management and Context API

State management is a fundamental aspect of building any dynamic web application. As your applications grow in complexity, effectively managing state becomes increasingly important. Next.js, in conjunction with React, provides various tools and patterns to help you manage state efficiently. Let's explore some advanced techniques.

5.1 Advanced Context API Usage

Alright, let's really get into the nitty-gritty of advanced Context API usage in React, and how it plays a role in Next.js applications. While Context API is often introduced as a simple way to avoid "prop drilling" (passing props down through many levels of a component tree), it's capable of much more. We can structure it for complex state management, and that's what we'll explore.

At its core, Context API provides a way to share data that can be considered "global" for a tree of React components. It's essentially a mechanism for components to subscribe to a value and be notified when that value changes.

The basic components of Context API are:

- createContext: This function returns a Context object. You use this object to provide and consume values.
- Context.Provider: A React component that allows consuming components to subscribe to context changes.
- Context.Consumer: A React component that subscribes to context changes.[1] (While still available, hooks like useContext are generally preferred now.)
- useContext: A React hook that allows function components to subscribe to context changes.

However, for advanced usage, we often move beyond simple value sharing. A very effective pattern is combining Context API with the useReducer hook. This combination allows us to manage more intricate state logic, similar to how Redux works, but without the overhead of a full-fledged library.

Let's illustrate this with a practical example: managing user authentication state.

JavaScript

```javascript
// contexts/AuthContext.js


import React, { createContext, useReducer,
useContext } from 'react';


const AuthStateContext = createContext(); // For
the state value

const AuthDispatchContext = createContext(); //
For the dispatch function


function authReducer(state, action) {

  switch (action.type) {

    case 'LOGIN':

      return { ...state, isAuthenticated: true,
user: action.payload };

    case 'LOGOUT':
```

```javascript
      return { ...state, isAuthenticated: false,
user: null };

    default:

      throw new Error(`Unhandled action type:
${action.type}`);

  }

}


export function AuthProvider({ children }) {

  const [state, dispatch] =
useReducer(authReducer, {

    isAuthenticated: false,

    user: null,

  });


  return (

    <AuthStateContext.Provider value={state}>

      <AuthDispatchContext.Provider
value={dispatch}>

        {children}

      </AuthDispatchContext.Provider>

    </AuthStateContext.Provider>
```

```javascript
  );

}


export function useAuthState() {

  const context = useContext(AuthStateContext);

  if (!context) {

    throw new Error('useAuthState must be used
within an AuthProvider');

  }

  return context;

}


export function useAuthDispatch() {

  const context =
useContext(AuthDispatchContext);

  if (!context) {

    throw new Error('useAuthDispatch must be used
within an AuthProvider');

  }

  return context;

}
```

Let's dissect this code:

1. Creating Contexts: We create two separate Contexts: AuthStateContext and AuthDispatchContext. This separation is a key part of the advanced pattern. AuthStateContext will hold the actual state values (like isAuthenticated and user), and AuthDispatchContext will hold the dispatch function that allows us to modify the state.

2. authReducer Function: The authReducer function is very similar to a Redux reducer. It takes the current state and an action, and returns the new state. It's responsible for updating the state based on the type of action dispatched.

3. AuthProvider Component: This component is the heart of our Context setup.
   - We use useReducer to create our state and dispatch function. The initial state is { isAuthenticated: false, user: null }.
   - We then provide the state to AuthStateContext.Provider and the dispatch function to AuthDispatchContext.Provider. This makes them available to any component nested within AuthProvider.
   - The children prop allows us to wrap any part of our component tree with this provider.

4. Custom Hooks (useAuthState, useAuthDispatch): These custom hooks are a crucial design pattern.
   - useAuthState uses useContext(AuthStateContext) to access the state.
   - useAuthDispatch uses useContext(AuthDispatchContext) to access the dispatch function.
   - Crucially, these hooks also perform a check to ensure that they are used within an AuthProvider. This helps prevent errors if a component tries to access the context without being wrapped in the provider.

Why is this pattern so powerful?

- Separation of Concerns: It cleanly separates the state data from the mechanism for updating it. Components that need to read the state use useAuthState, and components that need to modify the state use useAuthDispatch. This makes your code more predictable and easier to reason about.
- Performance Optimization: By separating the state and dispatch contexts, you can potentially optimize performance. If only the dispatch function changes, components that only consume the state may not need to re-render. (React's memoization techniques can further enhance this.)
- Scalability: This pattern scales well as your application grows. You can easily add more actions to your reducer and more state properties without making your components overly complex.

Real-world examples:

- Theme Management: You can use this pattern to manage the application's theme (light or dark mode). The state would include the current theme, and the actions would be like SET_THEME.
- Language Settings: You can manage the user's preferred language in a similar way.
- Shopping Cart: In an e-commerce application, you can manage the items in the user's shopping cart.

Exercise:

Let's solidify your understanding with an exercise. Create a context to manage a simple counter.

1. Create CounterContext.js.
2. Use useReducer to manage the counter value.
3. Implement actions for INCREMENT and DECREMENT.

4. Create CounterProvider, useCounterState, and useCounterDispatch hooks.
5. In a component, use the hooks to display the counter and provide buttons to increment and decrement it.

```javascript
// contexts/CounterContext.js


import React, { createContext, useReducer,
useContext } from 'react';


const CounterStateContext = createContext();

const CounterDispatchContext = createContext();


function counterReducer(state, action) {

  switch (action.type) {

    case 'INCREMENT':

      return { ...state, count: state.count + 1
};

    case 'DECREMENT':

      return { ...state, count: state.count - 1
};

    default:
```

```
      throw new Error(`Unhandled action type:
${action.type}`);

  }

}


export function CounterProvider({ children }) {

  const [state, dispatch] =
useReducer(counterReducer, { count: 0 });


  return (

    <CounterStateContext.Provider value={state}>

      <CounterDispatchContext.Provider
value={dispatch}>

        {children}

      </CounterDispatchContext.Provider>

    </CounterStateContext.Provider>

  );

}


export function useCounterState() {

  const context =
useContext(CounterStateContext);
```

```
  if (!context) {

    throw new Error('useCounterState must be used
within a CounterProvider');

  }

  return context;

}


export function useCounterDispatch() {

  const context =
useContext(CounterDispatchContext);

  if (!context) {

    throw new Error('useCounterDispatch must be
used within a CounterProvider');

  }

  return context;

}


// pages/counter.js (or any component)


import React from 'react';

import { useCounterState, useCounterDispatch,
CounterProvider } from
'../contexts/CounterContext';
```

```
function Counter() {

  const { count } = useCounterState();

  const dispatch = useCounterDispatch();


  return (

    <div>

      <h1>Count: {count}</h1>

      <button onClick={() => dispatch({ type:
'INCREMENT' })}>+</button>

      <button onClick={() => dispatch({ type:
'DECREMENT' })}>-</button>

    </div>

  );

}


function CounterPage() {

  return (

    <CounterProvider>

      <Counter />

    </CounterProvider>
```

```
    );

}
```

```
export default CounterPage;
```

This exercise will give you a solid foundation in using Context API with useReducer for advanced state management.

5.2 Integrating State Management Libraries (Redux, Zustand)

Okay, let's talk about integrating dedicated state management libraries into your Next.js applications. While Context API is powerful, for larger, more complex applications, you might find that libraries like Redux or Zustand provide a more structured and efficient way to manage your application's state.

Redux

Redux is a predictable state container for JavaScript apps.[1] It helps you write applications that behave consistently,[2] are easy to test, and can live in different environments (client, server, and native).[3]

Redux is based on three core principles:[4]

1. Single source of truth: The state of your entire application is stored in an object tree within a single store.[56] This makes it easier to inspect and debug your application's state.
2. State is read-only: The only way to change the state is to emit an action, an object describing what happened.[7] This ensures that neither the views nor the network callbacks will ever[8] directly write to the state.
3. Changes are made with pure functions: To specify how the state is transformed by actions, you write pure reducers.[9]

Pure reducers are functions that take the previous state and an action, and return the next state.[10]

Let's break down how to integrate Redux into a Next.js application.

Setting up the Redux Store:

First, you'll need to install Redux and react-redux (which provides bindings for React).

Bash

npm install redux react-redux

 # or

yarn add redux react-redux

Then, you create your Redux store.

This typically involves defining:

- Actions: Plain JavaScript objects that describe what happened.[11]
- Reducers: Pure functions that specify how the application's state changes in response to actions.[12]
- Store: The object that brings actions and reducers together.

```JavaScript
// store/store.js



import { createStore, combineReducers } from 'redux';
```

```
import counterReducer from
'./reducers/counterReducer'; // Assuming you have
a counterReducer


const rootReducer = combineReducers({

    counter: counterReducer,

});


const store = createStore(rootReducer);


export default store;
```

JavaScript

```
// store/reducers/counterReducer.js


const initialState = {

    value: 0,

};


function counterReducer(state = initialState,
action) {

    switch (action.type) {
```

```
        case 'COUNTER_INCREMENT':

            return { ...state, value: state.value
+ 1 };

        case 'COUNTER_DECREMENT':

            return { ...state, value: state.value
- 1 };

        default:

            return state;

    }

}


export default counterReducer;
```

Providing the Store to Your Application:

You need to make the Redux store available to all your components. You do this by using the Provider component from react-redux. Typically, you wrap your _app.js with the Provider.

```
JavaScript

// pages/_app.js


import React from 'react';

import { Provider } from 'react-redux';

import store from '../store/store'; // Your Redux store
```

```
import { PersistGate } from
'redux-persist/integration/react'; // If you're
using redux-persist

import { persistStore } from 'redux-persist'; //
If you're using redux-persist


let persistor = persistStore(store); // If you're
using redux-persist


function MyApp({ Component, pageProps }) {

    return (

        <Provider store={store}>

            <PersistGate loading={null}
persistor={persistor}>

                <Component {...pageProps} />

            </PersistGate>

        </Provider>

    );

}


export default MyApp;
```

Connecting Components to the Store:

To access the state and dispatch actions from your components, you use the useSelector and useDispatch hooks from react-redux.

- useSelector: Allows you to extract data from the Redux store state.
- useDispatch: Returns a reference to the dispatch function from the Redux store.[13]

JavaScript

```
// pages/counter.js



import React from 'react';

import { useSelector, useDispatch } from
'react-redux';



function Counter() {

    const count = useSelector((state) =>
state.counter.value); // Accessing the counter
value from the store

    const dispatch = useDispatch();


    return (

        <div>

            <h1>Counter: {count}</h1>
```

```
        <button onClick={() => dispatch({
type: 'COUNTER_INCREMENT' })}>Increment</button>

        <button onClick={() => dispatch({
type: 'COUNTER_DECREMENT' })}>Decrement</button>

    </div>

  );

}


export default Counter;
```

Zustand

Zustand is a small, fast, and scalable bearbones state-management solution.[14] It has a very simple API based on hooks and is often preferred for smaller to medium-sized applications where Redux might feel like overkill.

Installation:

Bash

npm install zustand

 # or

yarn add zustand

Creating a Store:

With Zustand, you create a store using the create function. Inside the create function, you define your state and actions.

```
JavaScript
```

```
// store/store.js

import create from 'zustand';

const useStore = create((set) => ({

    count: 0,

    increment: () => set((state) => ({ count:
state.count + 1 })),

    decrement: () => set((state) => ({ count:
state.count - 1 })),

}));

export default useStore;
```

Using the Store in Components:

To access the state and actions, you use the custom hook useStore in your components.

```
JavaScript

// pages/counter.js

import React from 'react';

import useStore from '../store/store';
```

```
function Counter() {

    const count = useStore((state) =>
state.count);

    const increment = useStore((state) =>
state.increment);

    const decrement = useStore((state) =>
state.decrement);


    return (

        <div>

            <h1>Counter: {count}</h1>

            <button
onClick={increment}>Increment</button>

            <button
onClick={decrement}>Decrement</button>

        </div>

    );

}


export default Counter;
```

Real-world examples:

- Redux: Best suited for large, complex applications with a lot of data and interactions.[15] Think of a large e-commerce platform or a complex enterprise application.

- Zustand: Excellent for medium-sized applications where simplicity and performance are key. A good example is a dashboard application or a single-page application with moderate complexity.

Exercise:

Create a simple shopping cart in Next.js using either Redux or Zustand. Implement functionality to:

- Add items to the cart.
- Remove items from the cart.
- Display the total price of the items in the cart.

This exercise will help you solidify your understanding of integrating state management libraries into Next.js.

5.3 Managing Complex Application State

Okay, let's tackle the topic of managing complex application state. This is where things get really interesting, and it's a skill that separates good developers from great ones. As your Next.js applications grow, you'll inevitably encounter scenarios where state management becomes a significant challenge. It's not just about storing data; it's about structuring it, updating it efficiently, and ensuring your application remains performant and maintainable.

Complex application state often involves:

- Nested data structures: Objects within objects, arrays within objects, and so on.
- Asynchronous updates: Data fetched from APIs, user interactions that trigger delayed changes.[1]
- Dependencies between state slices: One part of the state affecting another.

- Performance considerations: Avoiding unnecessary re-renders when only a small part of the state changes.

Here are some key strategies to effectively manage this complexity:

State Normalization

State normalization is a technique where you structure your state to minimize data duplication and improve data consistency. The core idea is to store data in a flat, relational structure, similar to how you would design a database.

Instead of nesting data, you store entities in separate objects, and you reference them by IDs.[2]

For example, consider an e-commerce application with products and categories.

A naive approach might be to nest categories within products:

```JavaScript
const state = {

    products: [

        {

            id: 1,

            name: 'Laptop',

            price: 1000,

            category: {

                id: 101,
```

```javascript
            name: 'Electronics',
        },
    },
    // ...
    ],
};
```

However, if you have multiple products in the same category, you're duplicating the category data.

A normalized state would look like this:

```javascript
JavaScript

const state = {
    products: {
        1: {
            id: 1,
            name: 'Laptop',
            price: 1000,
            category: 101, // Reference by ID
        },
        // ...
    },
    categories: {
```

```
    101: {

        id: 101,

        name: 'Electronics',

    },

    // ...

  },

};
```

Now, each category is stored only once, and products simply refer to the category by its ID. This makes updates easier and more efficient.

Immutable Updates

Immutable updates are crucial for maintaining predictability and improving performance.[3] In JavaScript, objects and arrays are mutable, meaning you can change them directly.[4] However, when you modify state directly, it can lead to unexpected side effects and make it difficult to track changes.

Immutable updates involve creating new objects and arrays instead of modifying the existing ones.[5] This ensures that the original state remains unchanged.

Here's an example of immutably updating an array:

```
JavaScript

const originalArray = [1, 2, 3];

const newArray = [...originalArray, 4]; // Create
a new array with 4 appended
```

```
// originalArray is still [1, 2, 3]
```

And here's how to immutably update an object:

JavaScript

```
const originalObject = { a: 1, b: 2 };

const newObject = { ...originalObject, c: 3 }; // Create a new object with c added

// originalObject is still { a: 1, b: 2 }
```

Libraries like Immer can simplify immutable updates by allowing you to work with a "draft" of the state, which Immer then immutably applies.[6]

Selectors

Selectors are functions that extract specific pieces of data from the application state.[7] They can also perform calculations or transformations on the data.

Selectors provide several benefits:

- Encapsulation: Components don't need to know the structure of the state. They only need to know how to use the selector.
- Memoization: Selectors can be memoized (cached) to avoid unnecessary recalculations. Libraries like Reselect can help with this.
- Performance: By selecting only the necessary data, you can prevent components from re-rendering when irrelevant parts of the state change.

Here's a simple example of a selector:

JavaScript

```javascript
const selectTotalPrice = (state) => {

    let total = 0;

    for (const itemId in state.cart.items) {

        total += state.cart.items[itemId].price *
state.cart.items[itemId].quantity;

    }

    return total;

};
```

This selector calculates the total price of items in a shopping cart.

Middleware (in Redux)

If you're using Redux, middleware provides a powerful way to handle asynchronous actions, logging, and other side effects.[8] Middleware sits between dispatching an action and the moment it reaches the reducer.

Common use cases for middleware:

- Asynchronous actions: Redux Thunk or Redux Saga allows you to dispatch actions that perform asynchronous operations, like fetching data from an API.[9]
- Logging: You can log actions and state changes for debugging purposes.
- Error handling: You can intercept errors and handle them centrally.

Here's a basic example of Redux Thunk:

JavaScript

```javascript
// actions/productActions.js
```

```javascript
export const fetchProducts = () => {

    return async (dispatch) => {

        dispatch({ type: 'FETCH_PRODUCTS_REQUEST'
});

        try {

            const response = await
fetch('/api/products');

            const data = await response.json();

            dispatch({ type:
'FETCH_PRODUCTS_SUCCESS', payload: data });

        } catch (error) {

            dispatch({ type:
'FETCH_PRODUCTS_FAILURE', payload: error.message
});

        }

    };

};
```

This action creator dispatches different actions based on the status of the asynchronous operation.

Real-world examples:

- E-commerce application: Managing product catalogs, shopping carts, user orders, and authentication state can become complex. Normalization, immutable updates, and selectors are crucial. Redux Thunk or Saga is essential for handling API calls.[10]

- Social media platform: Managing user profiles, posts, comments, and notifications involves nested data and frequent updates.[11] Efficient state management is critical for performance.[12]
- Complex dashboards: Dashboards with numerous widgets and real-time data require careful state structuring and optimization to avoid sluggish behavior.

Exercise:

Let's put these concepts into practice. Expand the shopping cart exercise from the previous section to include the following:

1. Normalization: Structure your cart state with normalized data, separating items and quantities.
2. Immutability: Ensure that all cart updates (adding, removing, changing quantities) are done immutably.
3. Selector: Create a selector to calculate the total price of items in the cart.
4. (If using Redux) Use Redux Thunk to simulate adding items to the cart asynchronously (e.g., fetching product details from an API).

This exercise will give you a solid foundation in handling complex application state in a Next.js application.

Chapter 6: Advanced Component Patterns and Optimization

React components are the building blocks of any Next.js application. Mastering advanced component patterns and optimization techniques is crucial for building scalable, maintainable, and performant applications. Let's explore some key concepts.

6.1 Higher-Order Components (HOCs) and Render Props

Okay, let's talk in detail about Higher-Order Components (HOCs) and Render Props. These are powerful patterns in React that allow you to reuse component logic. They're all about making your code more modular and preventing duplication, which is a huge win for maintainability and scalability.[1]

Higher-Order Components (HOCs)

A Higher-Order Component (HOC) is, essentially, a function that takes a component as an argument and returns a new, enhanced component.[2] It's like a component factory that can add extra features or functionality to existing components.

Think of it like this: You have a basic car. A HOC is like a customization shop. You bring your car to the shop, and they add things like a turbocharger, better brakes, or a fancy sound system. The shop doesn't change the original car; it creates a new, improved version.

HOCs are commonly used for:

- Sharing stateful logic: If several components need to manage the same state, a HOC can handle that logic and pass the state down as props.[3]

- Adding props: HOCs can inject specific props into components, providing them with data or functions.[4]
- Rendering hijacking: HOCs can control how a component is rendered, allowing you to conditionally render it, wrap it in other elements, or modify its output.[5]

Let's look at a practical example. Suppose you have several components that need to fetch data and display a loading indicator while the data is being fetched.

You can create a HOC to handle this:

JavaScript

```javascript
import React, { useState, useEffect } from
'react';



function withDataFetching(WrappedComponent, url)
{

  return function WithDataFetching(props) {

    const [data, setData] = useState(null);

    const [loading, setLoading] = useState(true);

    const [error, setError] = useState(null);


    useEffect(() => {

      setLoading(true);

      fetch(url)

        .then((response) => {
```

```
        if (!response.ok) {

            throw new Error('Network response was
not ok');

        }

        return response.json();

    })
    .then((data) => {

        setData(data);

        setLoading(false);

    })
    .catch((error) => {

        setError(error);

        setLoading(false);

    });
}, [url]);


if (loading) {

    return <div>Loading...</div>;

}


if (error) {
```

```jsx
    return <div>Error: {error.message}</div>;

  }


    return <WrappedComponent data={data}
{...props} />;

  };

}


function UserList({ data }) {

  return (

    <ul>

      {data.map((user) => (

        <li key={user.id}>{user.name}</li>

      ))}

    </ul>

  );

}


const UserListWithFetching = withDataFetching(

  UserList,

  'https://jsonplaceholder.typicode.com/users'
```

```
);
```

```
function MyPage() {

  return <UserListWithFetching />;

}
```

```
export default MyPage;
```

Here's how this HOC works:

1. withDataFetching is the HOC. It takes a WrappedComponent (the component you want to enhance) and a url (the API endpoint) as arguments.
2. It returns a new component, WithDataFetching. This new component manages the data fetching logic using useState and useEffect.
3. While the data is loading, it renders a "Loading..." message. If there's an error, it displays an error message.
4. Once the data is fetched, it renders the WrappedComponent, passing the fetched data as a prop. It also passes down any other props received by WithDataFetching using the spread syntax (...props).
5. UserList is a simple component that displays a list of users.
6. UserListWithFetching is created by applying the withDataFetching HOC to UserList.

This HOC allows you to reuse the data fetching logic in other components simply by wrapping them with withDataFetching.

Render Props

A Render Prop is a technique for sharing code between React components using a prop whose value is a function.[6] This function[7] (the "render prop") is called by the component that implements the logic, and it allows you to customize what is rendered.[8]

Think of it like this: You have a component that tracks the position of the mouse. Instead of the component itself rendering something specific, it provides the mouse coordinates to a function you give it, and you decide what to render with those coordinates.

Here's an example of a component that tracks the mouse position using a Render Prop:

JavaScript

```javascript
import React, { useState, useEffect } from
'react';


function MouseTracker({ children }) {

  const [position, setPosition] = useState({ x:
0, y: 0 });


  useEffect(() => {

    function handleMouseMove(event) {

      setPosition({ x: event.clientX, y:
event.clientY });

    }
```

```
    window.addEventListener('mousemove',
handleMouseMove);


    return () => {

      window.removeEventListener('mousemove',
handleMouseMove);

    };

  }, []);


  return children(position);

}


function MyComponent() {

  return (

    <MouseTracker>

      {(mouse) => (

        <p>

          Mouse position: ({mouse.x}, {mouse.y})

        </p>

      )}

    </MouseTracker>
```

```
  );

}
```

```
export default MyComponent;
```

Here's how this Render Prop works:

1. MouseTracker is the component that implements the mouse tracking logic. It uses useState to store the mouse position and useEffect to add and remove the mousemove event listener.
2. Instead of rendering something itself, it calls the children prop, passing the current mouse position as an argument.
3. MyComponent uses MouseTracker and provides a function as the children prop. This function receives the mouse position and renders the desired output.[9]

HOCs vs. Render Props

Both HOCs and Render Props solve the problem of code reuse, but they have some differences:

- HOCs wrap the component, while Render Props are used within the component's render method.[10]
- HOCs can sometimes lead to "wrapper hell" (deeply nested component trees), while Render Props are generally more straightforward to understand in the component tree.[11]
- HOCs can sometimes cause name collisions with props, while Render Props provide explicit access to the shared logic.[12]

Hooks and the Future

With the introduction of Hooks in React 16.8, many of the use cases for HOCs and Render Props can be achieved more simply and clearly. Hooks allow you to extract stateful logic into reusable functions, making your code more concise and easier to read.[13]

However, HOCs and Render Props are still valuable patterns to understand, especially when working with older codebases or libraries that haven't fully adopted Hooks.

Exercise:

Create a HOC or a Render Prop that provides a theme context to a component. The theme context should include properties like primaryColor and secondaryColor. Allow the component to access these theme properties.

Here's an example using a HOC:

JavaScript

```javascript
import React, { useState } from 'react';



const withTheme = (WrappedComponent) => {

  return function WithTheme(props) {

    const [theme] = useState({

      primaryColor: 'blue',

      secondaryColor: 'white',

    });



    return <WrappedComponent {...props}
theme={theme} />;
```

```
    };

};


function MyComponent({ theme }) {

  return (

    <div style={{ backgroundColor:
theme.primaryColor, color: theme.secondaryColor
}}>

      This is my component with a theme!

    </div>

  );

}


const ThemedComponent = withTheme(MyComponent);


function MyPage() {

  return <ThemedComponent />;

}


export default MyPage;
```

This exercise will help you solidify your understanding of HOCs and Render Props and how they can be used to share logic and functionality between components.

6.2 Code Splitting and Lazy Loading

Okay, let's have a detailed conversation about code splitting and lazy loading. These are crucial techniques for optimizing the performance of your Next.js applications, especially as they grow in complexity. They're all about delivering only the necessary code to the user, when they need it, which can significantly speed up initial page loads and improve overall user experience.

Code Splitting

Code splitting is the process of breaking down your application's code into smaller chunks that can be loaded on demand. Traditionally, when you build a web application, all your JavaScript code is bundled into one or a few large files. The browser has to download and parse these entire bundles before it can render the page, even if only a small portion of the code is actually needed for the initial view.

Code splitting addresses this by allowing you to split the code into smaller, more manageable chunks. The browser then only downloads the code that is required for the initial page load, and it can fetch other chunks as needed.

Next.js has built-in support for code splitting through dynamic import() statements. When you use import() as a function (instead of the standard static import), it tells Next.js to split the imported module into a separate chunk.

Let's illustrate this with an example. Suppose you have a component called HeavyComponent that contains a lot of code and is not needed for the initial render of your page.

You can lazy-load it using import():

JavaScript

```javascript
import React, { Suspense } from 'react';


const HeavyComponent = React.lazy(() =>
import('./HeavyComponent'));


function MyPage() {

  return (

    <div>

      <h1>My Page</h1>

      <Suspense fallback={<div>Loading...</div>}>

        <HeavyComponent />

      </Suspense>

    </div>

  );

}


export default MyPage;
```

Here's how this works:

1. React.lazy(): This function takes a function that calls import() and returns a Promise. The Promise resolves to the module with the component. React.lazy() only loads the component when it's rendered.
2. import('./HeavyComponent'): This is the dynamic import() statement. It tells Next.js to split HeavyComponent and its dependencies into a separate chunk.
3. Suspense: This React component lets you "suspend" the rendering of a component until its code is loaded. It takes a fallback prop, which specifies what to render while the component is loading.

When the user visits MyPage, Next.js will initially load only the code necessary to render MyPage itself. When HeavyComponent is about to be rendered, Next.js will fetch the separate chunk containing HeavyComponent and its dependencies. While this chunk is loading, the user will see the "Loading..." message.

Lazy Loading

Lazy loading is a technique that defers the loading of resources (like images, videos, or components) until they are needed. It's a specific form of code splitting, often applied to assets rather than JavaScript modules.

Lazy loading is particularly beneficial for improving the initial load time of pages with a lot of media content. Instead of downloading all images on the page when it first loads, you only download the images that are visible in the user's viewport. The rest of the images are loaded when the user scrolls down and they come into view.

Next.js provides built-in support for lazy loading images with the <Image> component from next/image. This component automatically optimizes and lazy-loads images.

Here's an example:

JavaScript

```
import Image from 'next/image';


function MyPage() {

  return (

    <div>

      <h1>My Page</h1>

      <Image

        src="/my-image.jpg"

        alt="My Image"

        width={500}

        height={300}

      />

      {/* Other content, including more images
*/}

    </div>

  );

}


export default MyPage;
```

The <Image> component does the following:

1. Lazy loading: It only loads the image when it's close to entering the viewport.
2. Optimization: It automatically optimizes the image to reduce its file size and improve loading performance.
3. Resizing: It can resize the image to fit the specified width and height, preventing layout shifts.

Real-World Examples

- E-commerce website: On a product page with many images and reviews, you can lazy-load the images and reviews that are below the fold (not immediately visible) to improve the initial loading speed.
- Social media platform: On a user's profile page with a long list of posts, you can lazy-load the posts as the user scrolls down, reducing the initial load time and improving performance.
- Single-Page Application (SPA): In a complex SPA with multiple routes, you can use dynamic import() to load the code for each route only when the user navigates to it.

Exercise

Create a page with a long list of components. Lazy-load each component as the user scrolls down. Use react-intersection-observer (a popular library for detecting when elements enter the viewport) to trigger the loading of each component.

```JavaScript
import React, { useState } from 'react';

import { useInView } from
'react-intersection-observer';
```

```
function LazyComponent({ index }) {

  const [loaded, setLoaded] = useState(false);

  const { ref, inView } = useInView();


  if (inView && !loaded) {

    // Simulate loading the component

    setTimeout(() => {

      setLoaded(true);

    }, 1000);

    return <div ref={ref}>Loading Component
{index}...</div>;

  }


  return (

    <div ref={ref}>

      {loaded ? <div>Component {index}
Loaded!</div> : <div>Placeholder for Component
{index}</div>}

    </div>

  );

}
```

```
function MyPage() {

  const components = Array.from({ length: 20 },
(_, i) => i + 1);


  return (

    <div>

      <h1>My Page</h1>

      {components.map((index) => (

        <LazyComponent key={index} index={index}
/>

      ))}

    </div>

  );

}
```

```
export default MyPage;
```

This exercise demonstrates how to use react-intersection-observer to trigger the loading of components when they come into view.

By mastering code splitting and lazy loading, you can build Next.js applications that are fast, efficient, and provide a great user experience, even with complex and resource-intensive content.

6.3 Optimizing Component Performance

Okay, let's talk about optimizing component performance in Next.js. This is where you really refine your application to be as smooth and responsive as possible. Even if your code is functional, inefficient components can lead to sluggishness and a poor user experience. We'll cover several key techniques to make your components run at their best.

Understanding the Problem: Unnecessary Re-renders

The main performance bottleneck in React applications often comes from unnecessary re-renders. React's virtual DOM is very efficient, but if a component re-renders when it doesn't need to, it can still cause performance issues, especially in complex applications.

React re-renders a component when:

- Its own state changes.
- Its props change.
- Its parent component re-renders.

The challenge is to prevent components from re-rendering when their props haven't actually changed.

Memoization with React.memo

React.memo is a Higher-Order Component (HOC) that can memoize a functional component. Memoization is a technique where the result of a function call is cached, and the function is only re-executed if its inputs change.

When you wrap a component with React.memo, React will only re-render it if its props have changed (using a shallow comparison).

Here's an example:

```javascript
import React, { useState } from 'react';


const MyComponent = React.memo(function
MyComponent(props) {

  console.log('Rendering MyComponent');

  return <div>{props.value}</div>;

});


function MyPage() {

  const [count, setCount] = useState(0);


  return (

    <div>

      <MyComponent value="Hello" />

      <button onClick={() => setCount(count +
1)}>Increment</button>

    </div>

  );

}
```

```javascript
export default MyPage;
```

In this case, MyComponent will only re-render if the value prop changes. Even though MyPage re-renders when the button is clicked, MyComponent won't re-render because its value prop remains "Hello". The console.log will help you see this in action.

You can also provide a custom comparison function to React.memo if you need more control over when the component should re-render:

JavaScript

```javascript
import React from 'react';



const MyComponent = React.memo(function
MyComponent(props) {

  console.log('Rendering MyComponent');

  return <div>{props.value.data}</div>;

}, (prevProps, nextProps) => {

  return prevProps.value.data ===
nextProps.value.data;

});



function MyPage() {

  const [data] = useState({ data: "Initial Data"
});
```

147

```javascript
  const [count, setCount] = useState(0);


  return (

    <div>

      <MyComponent value={data} />

      <button onClick={() => setCount(count +
1)}>Increment</button>

    </div>

  );

}


export default MyPage;
```

React.PureComponent (for Class Components)

React.PureComponent is similar to React.memo, but it's for class components. PureComponent implements shouldComponentUpdate with a shallow prop and state comparison. If the props and state haven't changed, the component won't re-render.

Here's an example:

```javascript
JavaScript

import React from 'react';


class MyComponent extends React.PureComponent {
```

```
  render() {

    console.log('Rendering MyComponent');

    return <div>{this.props.value}</div>;

  }

}


function MyPage() {

  const [count, setCount] = useState(0);


  return (

    <div>

      <MyComponent value="Hello" />

      <button onClick={() => setCount(count +
1)}>Increment</button>

    </div>

  );

}


export default MyPage;
```

MyComponent will only re-render if the value prop changes.

Virtualization for Large Lists

When you need to render very long lists (e.g., thousands or millions of items), rendering all the items at once can crush performance. Virtualization is a technique that only renders the items that are currently visible on the screen. As the user scrolls, new items are rendered, and old items are removed from the DOM.

Libraries like react-window and react-virtualized provide components for implementing virtualization.

Here's a basic example using react-window:

JavaScript

```javascript
import React from 'react';

import { FixedSizeList as List } from
'react-window';


const Row = ({ index, style }) => {

  return <div style={style}>Row {index}</div>;

};


function MyPage() {

  return (

    <div>

      <h1>Large List</h1>
```

```jsx
    <List height={150} itemCount={1000}
itemSize={35} width={300}>

       {Row}

    </List>

  </div>

  );

}


export default MyPage;
```

This code renders a list of 1000 rows, but only the rows that are visible within the 150px height are actually rendered.

Efficient State Updates

How you update your state can also significantly impact performance. Avoid unnecessary state updates and use functional updates when the new state depends on the previous state.

Here's an example of an inefficient state update:

```javascript
JavaScript

import React, { useState } from 'react';


function MyComponent() {

  const [items, setItems] = useState([]);
```

```javascript
// Inefficient: Creates a new array every time,
even if nothing changed

const addItem = (newItem) => {

  setItems([...items, newItem]);

};


return (

  <div>

    <button onClick={() => addItem({ id:
Date.now() })}>Add Item</button>

    <ul>

      {items.map(item => <li
key={item.id}>Item</li>)}

    </ul>

  </div>

);

}


export default MyComponent;
```

A more efficient approach is to use a functional update:

JavaScript

```javascript
import React, { useState } from 'react';
```

```
function MyComponent() {

  const [items, setItems] = useState([]);


  // Efficient: Only creates a new array if
addItem is actually called

  const addItem = (newItem) => {

    setItems(prevItems => [...prevItems,
newItem]);

  };


  return (

    <div>

      <button onClick={() => addItem({ id:
Date.now() })}>Add Item</button>

      <ul>

        {items.map(item => <li
key={item.id}>Item</li>)}

      </ul>

    </div>

  );

}
```

```
export default MyComponent;
```

Profiling with React DevTools

The React DevTools browser extension includes a Profiler tab that helps you identify performance bottlenecks in your components. It allows you to record how long it takes for each component to render and why components re-rendered. Use this tool to pinpoint and address performance issues.

Real-World Examples

- E-commerce website: Product listing pages often display a large number of products. Virtualization is essential to keep these pages performant.
- Data dashboards: Dashboards that display real-time data often need to update frequently. Memoization and efficient state updates are crucial to prevent the dashboard from becoming sluggish.
- Complex forms: Forms with many fields and dependencies can become slow if components re-render unnecessarily. React.memo and React.PureComponent can help optimize these forms.

Exercise

Create a component that displays a list of 10,000 items. Implement virtualization using react-window to optimize the rendering of the list.

```JavaScript
import React from 'react';

import { FixedSizeList as List } from
'react-window';
```

```
const Row = ({ index, style }) => {

  return <div style={style}>Item {index +
1}</div>;

};


function LargeList() {

  return (

    <div>

      <h1>Large List</h1>

      <List

        height={400}

        itemCount={10000}

        itemSize={50}

        width={300}

      >

        {Row}

      </List>

    </div>

  );

}
```

```
export default LargeList;
```

This exercise will give you practical experience in using virtualization to optimize the rendering of large lists.

By mastering these component optimization techniques, you can build Next.js applications that are not only feature-rich but also performant and provide a smooth, responsive user experience.

Chapter 7: Authentication and Authorization

Authentication and authorization are fundamental aspects of web development. They ensure that only authorized users can access specific resources and perform certain actions. Let's explore how to implement these concepts effectively in Next.js applications.

7.1 Best Practices for User Authentication

Okay, let's have a thorough discussion about user authentication. This is a cornerstone of web application security, and it's essential to get it right. I want to give you a solid understanding of how to authenticate users securely and effectively in your Next.js applications.

User authentication, at its core, is the process of verifying that someone is who they claim to be. It's like checking an ID before letting someone into a building or using a password to unlock your phone. In web applications, this usually involves verifying a user's credentials, such as a username and password, but it can also include other methods like social login or multi-factor authentication.

Let's break down the most important best practices to follow:

Use HTTPS Everywhere

This is non-negotiable. HTTPS (Hypertext Transfer Protocol Secure) encrypts the communication between the user's browser and your server. Without HTTPS, any data transmitted, including usernames and passwords, can be intercepted by anyone on the network. It's like sending a postcard versus sending a sealed letter.

In Next.js, you'll generally configure HTTPS at your hosting provider or with a reverse proxy like Nginx. Most modern hosting platforms (like Vercel, Netlify, etc.) provide HTTPS automatically. Make absolutely sure your site is always served over HTTPS.

Hash and Salt Passwords (Crucially!)

This is absolutely fundamental. You *never*, under any circumstances, store user passwords in plain text in your database. If your database is compromised, all your users' passwords are exposed.

Instead, you store a *hash* of the password. A hash is a one-way function. You can easily turn a password into a hash, but you can't easily reverse the process to get the original password back.

Here's how it works:

1. Hashing: You take the user's password and run it through a hashing algorithm. Popular choices include bcrypt, Argon2, and scrypt. These algorithms are designed to be computationally expensive, making it slow for attackers to try many password guesses.
2. Salting: Before hashing, you add a unique, random string called a "salt" to the password. This makes it even harder for attackers to use pre-computed tables of hashes (called "rainbow tables") to crack passwords.

Here's a simplified example of how you might hash and salt a password in a Next.js API route using bcrypt:

```
JavaScript


// pages/api/register.js



import bcrypt from 'bcrypt';
```

```javascript
import { v4 as uuidv4 } from 'uuid'; // For
generating unique IDs


export default async function handler(req, res) {

    if (req.method === 'POST') {

        const { email, password } = req.body;


        // Simulate checking if the email already
exists (replace with your database logic)
        const existingUser = null; // Assume no
user exists yet


        if (existingUser) {

            return res.status(400).json({
message: 'Email already in use' });

        }


        // Generate a salt

        const salt = await bcrypt.genSalt(10); //
10 is the "cost factor" - higher is slower but
more secure


        // Hash the password with the salt
```

```
        const hashedPassword = await
bcrypt.hash(password, salt);


        // Simulate saving the user to a database
(replace with your database logic)

        const newUser = {

            id: uuidv4(), // Generate a unique
user ID

            email,

            hashedPassword,

        };


        // ... (Save newUser to your database
here)


        res.status(201).json({ message: 'User
registered successfully' });

    } else {

        res.setHeader('Allow', ['POST']);

        res.status(405).end(`Method ${req.method}
Not Allowed`);

    }

}
```

Key Points about Hashing and Salting:

- Use a strong hashing algorithm: bcrypt and Argon2 are generally recommended.
- Use a high "cost factor" (for bcrypt) or similar setting in other algorithms. This controls how computationally expensive the hashing is. Higher cost = more secure, but slower to hash. Find a balance.
- Generate a new salt for each user. Don't use the same salt for everyone.
- Store *both* the salt and the hashed password in your database. You'll need the salt later to compare the stored hash with a newly entered password.

Secure Session Management

Once a user is authenticated (their credentials are verified), you need to keep track of their session so they don't have to log in on every page request. This is session management.

There are a few common approaches:

- Cookies: This is the most common method. The server sets a cookie in the user's browser, and the browser sends this cookie with every request. The server uses the cookie to identify the user.
- Local Storage (Use with Extreme Caution): Storing session tokens in local storage is generally *not recommended* for sensitive data like authentication tokens. Local storage is accessible to JavaScript, making it vulnerable to Cross-Site Scripting (XSS) attacks. If an attacker can inject malicious JavaScript into your site, they can steal the token.
- Server-Side Session Store: This involves storing session data on the server (e.g., in a database or cache). The server sends the user a session ID (usually in a cookie), and the server uses this ID to look up the session data. This is the most secure option but can be more complex to implement.

Here's an example of setting a secure cookie in a Next.js API route:

JavaScript

```
// pages/api/login.js (after successful
authentication)
```

```
import { serialize } from 'cookie';

import { v4 as uuidv4 } from 'uuid'; // For
generating session IDs
```

```
// ... (Authentication logic as shown before)
```

```
// Simulate creating a session

const sessionId = uuidv4(); // Generate a unique
session ID

// ... (Store sessionId and user data on the
server - e.g., in a database)
```

```
// Set the session cookie

const cookie = serialize('sessionId', sessionId,
{

    httpOnly: true, // Prevent client-side
JavaScript access
```

```
    secure: process.env.NODE_ENV ===
'production', // Only send over HTTPS

    sameSite: 'strict', // Protect against CSRF

    maxAge: 60 * 60 * 24 * 7, // 7 days (cookie
expiration)

    path: '/', // Cookie is valid for the whole
site

});



res.setHeader('Set-Cookie', cookie);

return res.status(200).json({ message: 'Login
successful' });
```

Cookie Security Flags:

- httpOnly: true: Prevents JavaScript from accessing the cookie. This significantly reduces the risk of XSS attacks.
- secure: true: (Important!) Only send the cookie over HTTPS.
- sameSite: 'strict': Provides strong protection against Cross-Site Request Forgery (CSRF) attacks.

Protect Against Common Attacks

- Cross-Site Scripting (XSS): This is a major threat. It involves an attacker injecting malicious JavaScript into your website, which can then steal user data, including session tokens.
    - Prevention: Sanitize user input rigorously. Use libraries like DOMPurify to prevent malicious HTML and JavaScript from being rendered. Use React's built-in escaping mechanisms (which are generally

good by default) to prevent injection when rendering user-provided strings.

- Cross-Site Request Forgery (CSRF): This attack tricks a user's browser into performing an unwanted action on your site while the user is authenticated.
  - Prevention: The sameSite: 'strict' cookie attribute helps a lot. You can also use anti-CSRF tokens (unique, unpredictable tokens that are included in form submissions).
- Brute-Force Attacks: Attackers try to guess user passwords by repeatedly trying different combinations.
  - Prevention: Implement rate limiting (e.g., limit the number of login attempts per IP address or user within a certain time frame). Consider using CAPTCHAs or similar challenges. Account lockout (temporarily disabling accounts after too many failed attempts) is also an option.

Use a Robust Authentication Library (Consider NextAuth.js)

Implementing authentication from scratch can be complex and error-prone. Libraries like next-auth can handle many of the complexities for you, including:

- Handling different authentication providers (e.g., username/password, social login).
- Session management.
- CSRF protection.

Using a well-vetted library can save you time and reduce the risk of security vulnerabilities.

Exercise:

Let's create a basic registration and login system in Next.js.

1. Create API routes for /api/register and /api/login.
2. In /api/register, handle POST requests, validate user input (email and password), hash and salt the password using bcrypt, and simulate saving the user to a database (you can use a simple in-memory store for this exercise).
3. In /api/login, handle POST requests, validate user input, simulate fetching the user from the database, compare the provided password with the stored hashed password using bcrypt, and set a secure session cookie upon successful authentication.
4. Create a simple UI with registration and login forms.

This exercise will give you a practical understanding of how to implement user authentication in Next.js.

7.2 Securing API Routes and Protecting Data

Okay, let's talk about securing your API routes and protecting data in Next.js. This is a crucial area because your API routes often handle sensitive information, and you need to ensure that only authorized users can access them and that the data is protected from unauthorized access or modification.

Think of your API routes as the back door to your house. You wouldn't leave that door unlocked, would you? Similarly, you need to put security measures in place to control who can access your API routes and what they can do.

Here are the key strategies to implement:

Authentication and Authorization

Authentication and authorization are the two pillars of securing API routes.

Authentication

As we discussed in the previous section, authentication is the process of verifying who the user is. You need to ensure that only logged-in users can access certain API routes.

Authorization

Authorization is the process of determining what an authenticated user is allowed to do. For example, an administrator might be allowed to delete users, while a regular user is not.

In Next.js API routes, you'll often use a combination of techniques to implement authentication and authorization:

- Session Management: You'll typically use session management (e.g., cookies, as discussed in the previous section) to identify authenticated users.
- Middleware: Next.js middleware can be used to intercept requests to API routes and check if the user is authenticated.
- Conditional Logic in API Routes: You can also add conditional logic within your API route handlers to check user roles or permissions.

Here's an example of using middleware to protect an API route:

```
JavaScript

// middleware.js


import { NextResponse } from 'next/server';
```

```javascript
import { verifySession } from './utils/auth'; //
Replace with your session verification logic


export async function middleware(req) {

    if
(req.nextUrl.pathname.startsWith('/api/admin')) {

        const sessionToken =
req.cookies.get('sessionToken')?.value;


        if (!sessionToken || !(await
verifySession(sessionToken))) {

            return NextResponse.json({ message:
'Unauthorized' }, { status: 401 });

        }


        // Simulate checking if the user is an
admin

        const sessionData = await
getSessionData(sessionToken); // Replace with
your logic

        if (!sessionData.isAdmin) {

            return NextResponse.json({ message:
'Forbidden' }, { status: 403 });

        }
```

```
    }


    return NextResponse.next();

}


export const config = {

    matcher: '/api/admin/:path*',

};


// utils/auth.js (Example - Replace with your
actual implementation)

// This is a placeholder. You'll need to define
your own logic for verifying sessions.

// This could involve checking a database,
verifying a JWT, etc.

export async function verifySession(sessionToken)
{

    // Replace this with your actual session
verification logic

    // For example, you might:

    // 1. Verify a JWT

    // 2. Check if the session token exists in a
database
```

```
// 3. etc.

    return true; // Placeholder: Always returns
true (for demonstration only!)

}



// utils/auth.js (Example - Replace with your
actual implementation)

export async function
getSessionData(sessionToken) {

    // Replace this with your actual logic to
retrieve session data

    // based on the session token.

    // This could involve querying a database or
decoding a JWT.

    return { isAdmin: true }; // Placeholder:
Always returns true (for demonstration only!)

}



// pages/api/admin/users.js


export default async function handler(req, res) {

    // This route is protected by the middleware

    const users = [
```

```
    { id: 1, name: 'Admin User' },

    { id: 2, name: 'Another User' },

  ];

  res.status(200).json(users);

}
```

In this example:

- The middleware.js file intercepts requests to any route under /api/admin/.
- It checks for a sessionToken cookie. If it's missing or invalid, it returns a 401 Unauthorized response.
- It then simulates checking if the user associated with the session is an administrator. If not, it returns a 403 Forbidden response.
- The /api/admin/users.js route is only accessible to authenticated administrators.

Input Validation

Always, without exception, validate and sanitize user input. This is absolutely critical to prevent various security vulnerabilities:

- Injection Attacks: These attacks involve injecting malicious code (e.g., SQL, JavaScript) into your application through user input fields.
  - SQL Injection: Attackers can manipulate database queries by injecting SQL code into input fields.
  - Cross-Site Scripting (XSS): Attackers can inject malicious JavaScript into your website, which can then steal user data or perform other harmful actions.

- Buffer Overflow: In some cases, attackers can provide overly long input that causes your application to crash or behave unexpectedly.

Here's how to approach input validation:

- Server-Side Validation: *Always* perform validation on the server. Client-side validation is helpful for providing immediate feedback to the user, but it can be bypassed.
- Whitelisting: Define what *valid* input looks like and reject anything that doesn't match. Don't try to blacklist specific characters or patterns, as attackers are very clever at finding ways around blacklists.
- Sanitization: Sanitize user input to remove or escape potentially harmful characters. For example, if you're displaying user-provided HTML, use a library like DOMPurify to remove any malicious code.
- Libraries: Consider using libraries like Joi or Yup to define validation schemas.

Here's an example of input validation in a Next.js API route:

JavaScript

```
// pages/api/posts.js



import { validate } from 'uuid'; // Example: For
validating UUIDs



export default function handler(req, res) {

    if (req.method === 'POST') {
```

```javascript
        const { title, content, authorId } =
req.body;



        if (!title || typeof title !== 'string'
|| title.trim().length === 0) {

        return res.status(400).json({
message: 'Title is required' });

        }



        if (!content || typeof content !==
'string' || content.trim().length === 0) {

        return res.status(400).json({
message: 'Content is required' });

        }



        if (!authorId || typeof authorId !==
'string' || !validate(authorId)) {

        return res.status(400).json({
message: 'Invalid authorId' });

        }



        // Simulate saving the post to a database
(replace with your logic)
```

```
        const newPost = { id: Date.now(), title,
content, authorId };

        res.status(201).json(newPost);

    } else {

        res.setHeader('Allow', ['POST']);

        res.status(405).end(`Method ${req.method}
Not Allowed`);

    }

}
```

Rate Limiting

Rate limiting is a technique that limits the number of requests that a user or client can make to your API within a given time period.

This is essential to:

- Prevent Brute-Force Attacks: Attackers often try to guess passwords by repeatedly sending login requests. Rate limiting can slow them down or block them.
- Prevent Denial-of-Service (DoS) Attacks: Attackers can flood your API with requests, making it unavailable to legitimate users.
- Protect Your Resources: Rate limiting can help prevent abuse of your API and protect your server resources.

You can implement rate limiting using libraries like express-rate-limit (if you're using a custom server) or by using rate limiting features provided by your hosting platform.

Here's a conceptual example (you'll need to adapt it to your specific setup):

JavaScript

```javascript
// (Conceptual example - Adapt to your setup)


const rateLimit = require('express-rate-limit');
// If using a custom server


const apiLimiter = rateLimit({

    windowMs: 15 * 60 * 1000, // 15 minutes

    max: 100, // Limit each IP to 100 requests
per windowMs

    message: 'Too many requests, please try again
later.',

});


// (In your custom server setup)

// server.use('/api/', apiLimiter);


// (Or, you might implement simple rate limiting
within your API route)

// pages/api/my-api-route.js
```

```javascript
const requestCounts = new Map(); // Store request
counts (e.g., per IP)


export default function handler(req, res) {

    const clientIp =
req.headers['x-forwarded-for'] ||
req.connection.remoteAddress; // Get client's IP


    if (!requestCounts.has(clientIp)) {

        requestCounts.set(clientIp, { count: 0,
lastRequestTime: Date.now() });

    }


    const clientData =
requestCounts.get(clientIp);

    const now = Date.now();


    if (now - clientData.lastRequestTime > 60000)
{ // 1 minute window

        clientData.count = 0;

        clientData.lastRequestTime = now;

    }
```

```
    if (clientData.count >= 10) { // Allow 10
requests per minute

        return res.status(429).json({ message:
'Too many requests' });

    }



    clientData.count++;

    // ... (Your API logic here)

}
```

Data Encryption

Encrypting sensitive data is another critical layer of protection.

- Encryption at Rest: Encrypt sensitive data stored in your database. This means that even if someone gains unauthorized access to your database files, the data will be unreadable without the decryption key.
- Encryption in Transit: As we discussed earlier, always use HTTPS to encrypt data while it's being transmitted between the client and the server.

For database encryption, your database system will usually provide encryption features.

Regular Security Audits

Security is an ongoing process. You should conduct regular security audits to identify and address potential vulnerabilities in your Next.js application.

- Penetration Testing: Consider hiring a security professional to perform penetration testing, where they simulate real-world attacks to find weaknesses.
- Code Reviews: Have your code reviewed by other developers to identify potential security flaws.
- Stay Updated: Keep your Next.js, React, and all other dependencies up to date. Security vulnerabilities are often discovered and patched, so it's essential to stay current.

Exercise:

Let's create a simple API route with authentication and input validation.

1. Create an API route /api/posts.
2. Protect this route so that only authenticated users can create posts. (You can simulate authentication for this exercise, e.g., by checking for a specific header or cookie).
3. The route should accept a POST request with title and content in the request body.
4. Validate the title and content to ensure they are strings and not empty.
5. Return a 401 Unauthorized response if the user is not authenticated.
6. Return a 400 Bad Request response if the input data is invalid.
7. If the input data is valid and the user is authenticated, simulate saving the post and return a 201 Created response.

This exercise will help you understand how to protect API routes and validate user input in Next.js.

7.3 Integrating Authentication Providers (Auth0, Firebase)

Okay, let's discuss integrating authentication providers like Auth0 and Firebase into your Next.js applications. This is a very common and often highly recommended approach because these providers handle a lot of the complexity of authentication for you, allowing you to focus on building your application's core features.

Authentication providers essentially offer "authentication as a service." They take care of user registration, login, password management, and often many other related features. This not only saves you development time but also significantly improves the security of your application, as these providers are experts in handling authentication securely.

Let's explore some of the key benefits of using these providers and how to integrate them.

Benefits of Using Authentication Providers

- Reduced Development Effort: You don't have to write code to handle password hashing, session management, and other authentication-related tasks. This can save you a lot of time and effort.
- Improved Security: Authentication providers have robust security practices and infrastructure, which can help protect your application from common security vulnerabilities. They keep up with the latest security best practices, so you don't have to.
- Enhanced User Experience: They often offer features like social login (login with Google, Facebook, etc.), passwordless authentication, and multi-factor authentication, which can improve the user experience.

- Scalability: Authentication providers are designed to handle a large number of users and requests, so they can scale with your application.
- Feature Richness: Many providers offer additional features like user management, authorization, and analytics, which can be useful for managing your application.

Popular Authentication Providers

- Auth0: A flexible and feature-rich platform that supports various authentication methods and identity providers. It's highly customizable and suitable for complex applications.
- Firebase Authentication: Part of the Firebase platform, it provides easy-to-use authentication services with strong integration with other Firebase services. It's often favored for applications already using Firebase.

Integrating with Next.js using next-auth

A popular library that simplifies the integration with various authentication providers in Next.js is next-auth. It handles a lot of the underlying complexity, making it easier to add authentication to your application.

Let's walk through a basic example of integrating next-auth with Google as the authentication provider.

Installation

First, you need to install next-auth:

Bash

npm install next-auth

or

yarn add next-auth

Setting up the Auth API Route

next-auth uses a special API route to handle authentication requests. You create this route in pages/api/auth/[...nextauth].js:

JavaScript

```javascript
// pages/api/auth/[...nextauth].js


import NextAuth from 'next-auth';

import GoogleProvider from
'next-auth/providers/google';


export default NextAuth({

    providers: [

        GoogleProvider({

            clientId:
process.env.GOOGLE_CLIENT_ID,

            clientSecret:
process.env.GOOGLE_CLIENT_SECRET,

        }),

    ],

    secret: process.env.NEXTAUTH_SECRET,

    callbacks: {

        async session({ session, token, user }) {
```

```
        // Send properties to the client,
like an access_token from a provider.

        session.accessToken =
token.accessToken;

        return session;

      },

    },

    // Add callbacks, events, etc. as needed

});
```

Here's a breakdown:

- NextAuth: This is the main function from the next-auth library.
- providers: This array configures the authentication providers you want to use. In this case, we're using GoogleProvider.
- clientId and clientSecret: These are credentials you obtain from the Google Cloud Console when you set up your Google OAuth 2.0 application.
- process.env.GOOGLE_CLIENT_ID and process.env.GOOGLE_CLIENT_SECRET: It's crucial to store these sensitive values in environment variables and *never* expose them in your client-side code.
- secret: This is a secret used to encrypt tokens. Store it securely in an environment variable (process.env.NEXTAUTH_SECRET).
- callbacks: This allows you to customize how the authentication process works. The session callback is useful for adding extra properties to the session object.

Environment Variables

You'll need to set up the necessary environment variables. Create a .env.local file in your project root and add the following:

GOOGLE_CLIENT_ID=YOUR_GOOGLE_CLIENT_ID

GOOGLE_CLIENT_SECRET=YOUR_GOOGLE_CLIENT_SECRET

NEXTAUTH_SECRET=YOUR_NEXTAUTH_SECRET

NEXTAUTH_URL=http://localhost:3000 // Or your production URL

Replace YOUR_GOOGLE_CLIENT_ID, YOUR_GOOGLE_CLIENT_SECRET, and YOUR_NEXTAUTH_SECRET with the actual values.

NEXTAUTH_URL should be your application's URL. This is important for generating correct callback URLs.

Using useSession to Access Session Data

In your components, you can use the useSession hook from next-auth/react to access the user's session data:

JavaScript

```
// pages/profile.js
```

```
import { useSession, signIn, signOut } from
'next-auth/react';
```

```
function Profile() {

    const { data: session } = useSession();


    if (session) {

        return (

            <div>

                <p>Welcome,
{session.user.email}!</p>

                <button onClick={() =>
signOut()}>Sign out</button>

            </div>

        );

    }

    return (

        <div>

            <p>Not signed in</p>

            <button onClick={() => signIn()}>Sign
in</button>

        </div>

    );

}
```

```
export default Profile;
```

- useSession: This hook provides access to the session object. If the user is signed in, session will contain information about the user. If the user is not signed in, session will be null.
- signIn and signOut: These functions allow you to initiate the sign-in and sign-out flows.

Protecting Pages or API Routes

You can protect pages or API routes by checking the session status.

For example, to protect a page using getServerSideProps:

JavaScript

```javascript
// pages/protected.js


import { getSession } from 'next-auth/react';


function ProtectedPage() {

    return (

        <div>

            <h1>Protected Page</h1>

            <p>This page is only accessible to
signed-in users.</p>

        </div>

    );
```

```javascript
}


export async function getServerSideProps(context)
{

    const session = await getSession(context);


    if (!session) {

        return {

            redirect: {

                destination: '/api/auth/signin',

                permanent: false,

            },

        };

    }


    return {

        props: {},

    };

}


export default ProtectedPage;
```

- getSession: This function allows you to access the session in getServerSideProps.
- If getSession returns null (no session), we redirect the user to the sign-in page.

Real-World Examples

- E-commerce application: You'd use authentication to manage user accounts, orders, and payment information.
- Social media platform: Authentication is essential for user profiles, posts, comments, and messaging.
- SaaS application: Any application with user-specific data or features requires robust authentication.

Exercise

1. Set up next-auth in a Next.js application.
2. Integrate with a provider of your choice (e.g., GitHub, Credentials for username/password).
3. Create a "profile" page that displays the user's information if they are signed in, and a sign-in button if they are not.
4. Protect an API route or a page so that only authenticated users can access it.

This exercise will give you practical experience in integrating an authentication provider with Next.js using next-auth.

Chapter 8: Performance Optimization and Best Practices

Performance is a crucial aspect of any web application. Users expect fast and responsive experiences, and search engines prioritize websites with good performance. Next.js provides many tools and techniques to help you optimize your applications. Let's explore them in detail.

8.1 Image Optimization and Asset Management

Okay, let's have a really in-depth discussion about image optimization and asset management within the context of Next.js. This is a critical area for web performance, and Next.js gives you some excellent tools to handle it. It's not just about making your site look good; it's about making it load fast and provide a smooth experience.

Image Optimization with next/image

Let's start with images, as they often represent a significant portion of the data that needs to be downloaded when a user visits a web page. If you don't handle them carefully, they can become a major bottleneck.

Next.js provides the <Image> component from next/image, which is a powerful and recommended way to work with images. It's designed to optimize images automatically, making your site faster and more efficient.

Here's why next/image is so important:

- Lazy Loading: This is a fundamental optimization technique. Instead of downloading all images on a page when it initially loads, next/image defers loading images until they are close to entering the viewport. The viewport is the area of the web page that is currently visible to the user in their browser. This means that images below the fold (the part of the page the user has to scroll to see) are only loaded when the user scrolls down. This dramatically reduces the initial load time, especially on pages with many images.

- Automatic Optimization: next/image can automatically optimize images to reduce their file size. It does this by using modern image formats like WebP (if the user's browser supports it), which often provides better compression than older formats like JPEG. It can also adjust the quality of the image to find the right balance between file size and visual fidelity. This can lead to significant savings in bandwidth and faster loading times.
- Resizing: When you display an image on your page, you need to ensure that it's sized correctly to avoid layout shifts. Layout shifts occur when elements on the page move around as images load, which can be a jarring experience for users. next/image helps prevent this by allowing you to specify the width and height of the image. It will then ensure that the correct amount of space is reserved for the image, even before it has finished loading.

Let's see a code example:

```javascript
JavaScript


import Image from 'next/image';


function MyComponent() {

  return (

    <div>
```

```
    <h1>My Page</h1>

    <Image

      src="/my-image.jpg"

      alt="A detailed description of the image"

      width={500}

      height={300}

    />

  </div>

  );

}


export default MyComponent;
```

Here's what's happening in this code:

1. import Image from 'next/image';: We import the Image component from the next/image library.
2. <Image src="/my-image.jpg" ... />: We use the Image component to display our image.
3. src="/my-image.jpg": This specifies the source of the image. A key point here is that for optimal performance, you should place your static images in the public directory of your Next.js project. Next.js is optimized to serve images from this directory.
4. alt="A detailed description of the image": The alt attribute is extremely important. It provides a text description of the image, which is crucial for:

- Accessibility: Screen readers use the alt text to describe images to users with visual impairments.
- SEO: Search engines use the alt text to understand the content of images, which can improve your website's search engine ranking.
5. width={500} height={300}: These attributes tell next/image the intended dimensions of the image. This allows Next.js to:
   - Resize the image appropriately.
   - Reserve the correct amount of space on the page to prevent layout shifts.

Important Nuances of next/image

- Image Placement: As mentioned, for static images that are part of your application's design, placing them in the public directory is the recommended approach. This allows Next.js to efficiently serve and optimize them.
- Layout Shifts and width/height: Always provide the width and height attributes to the Image component. This is essential for preventing layout shifts. If you don't know the exact dimensions, you can use the layout prop to control how the image is scaled.
- Image Optimization Configuration: You can customize how Next.js optimizes images by adjusting settings in your next.config.js file. For example, you can specify the domains of external image sources that you want Next.js to optimize.
- Remote Images: next/image can also handle images hosted on external servers. However, you need to add the domains of these external servers to the domains array within the images configuration in your next.config.js file.

Beyond Images: Asset Management

While images are a significant part of asset management, it's important to consider other types of assets as well, such as:

- CSS (Cascading Style Sheets): These files control the visual presentation of your web pages.
- JavaScript: These files contain the code that makes your web pages interactive.
- Fonts: These files define the typography used on your web pages.

Here are some general principles of good asset management:

- Bundling: Next.js (under the hood, Webpack does this) bundles your JavaScript and CSS files. Bundling combines multiple files into fewer files. This is important because each file the browser has to download requires an HTTP request. Fewer HTTP requests generally mean faster loading times.
- Minification: Next.js also minifies your CSS and JavaScript. Minification removes unnecessary characters from your code, such as whitespace, comments, and line breaks. This reduces the file size, which makes the files download faster.
- Caching: Caching is a technique that allows the browser to store copies of your assets. When the user visits your site again, the browser can load the assets from its cache instead of downloading them again, which significantly improves performance. Next.js provides some built-in caching mechanisms, but you might need to configure caching headers for more fine-grained control.
- Content Delivery Networks (CDNs): CDNs are networks of servers distributed around the world. They store copies of your assets, and when a user requests an asset, it's served from the server that's closest to them. This reduces latency (the time it takes for data to travel from the server to the

user's browser) and improves loading times, especially for users who are geographically distant from your main server.

Exercise

Let's create a Next.js page that displays a gallery of images using next/image.

1. Place a few images in your public/images directory. You can name them image1.jpg, image2.jpg, etc.
2. Create a new page (e.g., pages/gallery.js).
3. In this page, use the Image component to display the images.
4. Make sure to:
   ○ Set the src attribute to the correct path of each image.
   ○ Provide meaningful alt attributes.
   ○ Specify the width and height of each image.

Here's a starting point for your code:

JavaScript

```javascript
import Image from 'next/image';



function ImageGallery() {

  return (

    <div>

      <h1>Image Gallery</h1>

      <div style={{ display: 'flex', flexWrap:
'wrap' }}>
```

```
<Image

  src="/images/image1.jpg"

  alt="A scenic landscape"

  width={300}

  height={200}

  style={{ margin: '10px' }}

/>

<Image

  src="/images/image2.jpg"

  alt="A close-up of a flower"

  width={300}

  height={200}

  style={{ margin: '10px' }}

/>

<Image

  src="/images/image3.jpg"

  alt="A cityscape at night"

  width={300}

  height={200}

  style={{ margin: '10px' }}
```

```
        />

        {/* Add more Image components for your
other images */}

      </div>

   </div>

  );

}
```

```
export default ImageGallery;
```

This exercise will give you practical experience in using the next/image component and managing images in a Next.js application.

By understanding and implementing effective image optimization and asset management techniques, you can build Next.js applications that are not only visually appealing but also fast, efficient, and provide a great user experience.

8.2 Performance Monitoring and Measurement

Okay, let's have a really detailed discussion about performance monitoring and measurement in the context of Next.js. This is a crucial area because you can't truly optimize what you don't measure. Understanding how your application performs, identifying bottlenecks, and tracking improvements is essential for delivering a great user experience.

Think of it like going to the doctor for a checkup. You wouldn't just guess if you're healthy; you'd run tests, measure vital signs, and track your progress over time. The same applies to your web application.

Here are the key areas we'll cover:

Web Vitals

Web Vitals are a set of standardized metrics defined by Google that aim to quantify the core aspects of user experience on the web.

They focus on three key areas:

- Largest Contentful Paint (LCP): This measures how long it takes for the largest content element (like an image or text block) to become visible within the viewport. A good LCP[1] helps users feel like the page loaded quickly.
- First Input Delay (FID): This measures the time from when a user first interacts with your page (like clicking a button or link) to when the browser is actually able to begin processing event handlers in response to that interaction. A low FID ensures that your page is responsive to user input.
- Cumulative Layout Shift (CLS): This measures the amount of unexpected layout shifts that occur during the page's loading phase. Layout shifts are those annoying moments when elements on the page move around while you're trying to read or interact with them. A low CLS provides a more stable and predictable visual experience.

Next.js provides built-in support for reporting Web Vitals. You can use the reportWebVitals function in your pages/_app.js file to collect these metrics:

```JavaScript
// pages/_app.js
```

```
import React from 'react';


function MyApp({ Component, pageProps }) {

    return <Component {...pageProps} />;

}


export function reportWebVitals(metric) {

    console.log(metric);

    // Send these metrics to an analytics service

    // Example:

    // if (metric.name === 'LCP') {

    //      // ...

    // }

    // if (metric.name === 'FID') {

    //      // ...

    // }

    // if (metric.name === 'CLS') {

    //      // ...

    // }
```

```
}
```

```
export default MyApp;
```

Here's how this works:

- reportWebVitals(metric): This function is automatically called by Next.js when a Web Vitals metric is ready to be reported.
- The metric object contains information about the specific metric (e.g., metric.name, metric.value).
- Inside reportWebVitals, you'll typically want to send these metrics to an analytics service (like Google Analytics, or a dedicated performance monitoring service) so you can track them over time and identify areas for improvement.

Why are Web Vitals important?

- User Experience: They directly correlate with how users perceive the performance of your website.
- SEO: Search engines like Google use Web Vitals as a ranking factor.
- Standardization: They provide a common language and set of metrics for discussing web performance.

Browser Developer Tools

Modern browsers have powerful developer tools that provide a wealth of information about your website's performance. Here are some key areas to explore:

- Network Tab: This tab shows you all the resources that the browser downloads (HTML, CSS, JavaScript, images, etc.). You can see how long each resource takes to download, the size of the resources, and the order in which they are downloaded. This is invaluable for identifying bottlenecks.

- Performance Tab: This tab allows you to record a performance profile of your page. You can see how long it takes for the browser to parse HTML, execute JavaScript, render the page, and perform other tasks. This helps you pinpoint which parts of your code are slow.
- Lighthouse: Chrome's Lighthouse tool provides automated auditing for performance, accessibility, best practices, SEO, and Progressive Web Apps (PWAs). It gives you a score for each of these areas and provides recommendations for improvement.

Example: Using the Chrome Performance Tab

1. Open Chrome Developer Tools (usually by pressing F12 or right-clicking on the page and selecting "Inspect").
2. Go to the "Performance" tab.
3. Click the "Record" button (the circular button) and then reload the page.
4. Let the page load completely and then click the "Stop" button.
5. Chrome will now show you a detailed performance profile. You can zoom in on different areas, examine the timeline, and see how long each operation took.

Real User Monitoring (RUM)

While developer tools are great for testing in a controlled environment, Real User Monitoring (RUM) allows you to collect performance data from *real users* who are visiting your website. This gives you a much more accurate picture of how your site performs in the wild, under various network conditions and on different devices.

RUM tools typically collect data such as:

- Page load times.
- Time to first byte (TTFB).

- JavaScript execution times.
- Error rates.
- Geographic location of users.
- Device types and browsers used by users.

You can use dedicated RUM services or implement your own basic RUM solution by collecting data using JavaScript and sending it to your server.

Logging and Error Tracking

Monitoring your server logs and tracking JavaScript errors is crucial for identifying performance issues and other problems.

- Server Logs: Server logs can provide valuable information about server response times, errors, and other server-side performance metrics.
- Error Tracking: Services like Sentry or Bugsnag help you track JavaScript errors that occur in the browser. These services can provide detailed information about the errors, including stack traces, user context, and browser information.

Exercise

1. Create a Next.js page with some content (text, an image, etc.).
2. Use the Chrome Developer Tools to:
    - Examine the Network tab and see how long it takes to download the page's resources.
    - Use the Performance tab to record a performance profile and identify any performance bottlenecks.
    - Use Lighthouse to audit the page and see its performance score.
3. Implement reportWebVitals in your _app.js and add some code to log the Web Vitals metrics to the console.

This exercise will give you practical experience in using browser developer tools and Next.js's Web Vitals reporting to monitor and measure your application's performance.

8.3 Advanced Optimization Techniques

Okay, let's talk about some advanced optimization techniques in Next.js. We've covered the fundamentals, but to really squeeze out every bit of performance and build truly exceptional applications, we need to go a bit deeper. These techniques can sometimes be a bit more complex, but they're incredibly powerful when applied correctly.

Code Splitting

Code splitting is a technique where you break down your application's code into smaller chunks that can be loaded on demand. This is a game-changer because browsers don't have to download the entire application's code upfront. They only download the code that's needed for the initial page load, and then they can fetch other chunks as the user navigates or interacts with the application.

Next.js has excellent built-in support for code splitting. The primary way you achieve this is using dynamic import() statements.

Here's how dynamic import() works:

Instead of the standard static import (e.g., import MyComponent from './MyComponent';), you use import() as a function:

JavaScript

```
const MyComponent = React.lazy(() =>
import('./MyComponent'));
```

- import('./MyComponent'): This returns a Promise that resolves to the module containing MyComponent.
- React.lazy(): This is a React function that lets you render a dynamic import as a regular component. It takes a function that calls import() and returns a React component that loads the other component when it's rendered.

To handle the loading state while the component is being fetched, you use the <Suspense> component:

JavaScript

```
import React, { Suspense } from 'react';



const MyComponent = React.lazy(() =>
import('./MyComponent'));



function MyPage() {

    return (

        <div>

            <h1>My Page</h1>

            <Suspense
fallback={<div>Loading...</div>}>

                <MyComponent />

            </Suspense>

        </div>

    );
```

```
}
```

```
export default MyPage;
```

> \<Suspense fallback={\<div>Loading...\</div>}>: This component displays the fallback content (in this case, "Loading...") while MyComponent is being loaded. Once MyComponent and its dependencies are loaded, Suspense renders MyComponent.

Why is code splitting so effective?

- Faster Initial Load: Users see the initial page content sooner because the browser doesn't have to download a massive JavaScript bundle.
- Improved Performance: The browser only executes the code that's needed for the current view, reducing the workload and improving responsiveness.
- Better User Experience: Users feel like the application is faster and more interactive.

Code Splitting Patterns in Next.js:

- Route-Based Splitting: Next.js automatically code-splits your application based on your pages directory. Each page becomes a separate bundle.
- Component-Based Splitting: You can use React.lazy() and dynamic import() to split individual components, as shown in the example above.

Memoization

Memoization is a technique where you cache the results of expensive function calls and return the cached result when the same inputs occur[1] again. This prevents you from repeating the same calculations unnecessarily.

React provides a few tools for memoization:

React.memo: This is a Higher-Order Component (HOC) that memoizes a functional component. It performs a shallow comparison of the component's props and only re-renders the component if the props have changed.

```javascript
import React from 'react';


const MyComponent = React.memo(function
MyComponent(props) {

    console.log('Rendering MyComponent');

    return <div>{props.value}</div>;

});


function MyPage() {

    const [count, setCount] = React.useState(0);


    return (

        <div>

            <MyComponent value="Hello" />
```

```
        <button onClick={() => setCount(count
+ 1)}>Increment</button>

        </div>

    );

}
```

```
export default MyPage;
```

In this example, MyComponent will only re-render if the value prop changes. Even though MyPage re-renders when the button is clicked, MyComponent won't re-render because its value prop remains "Hello".

useMemo: This is a React Hook that memoizes the result of a function. You provide a function and an array of dependencies to useMemo. useMemo will only re-run the function when one of the dependencies changes.

```
JavaScript
```

```
import React from 'react';
```

```
function MyComponent(props) {

    const expensiveValue = React.useMemo(() => {

        // Perform expensive calculation here
```

```
        console.log('Calculating expensive
value');

        return props.data * 2;

    }, [props.data]);


    return <div>{expensiveValue}</div>;

}



function MyPage() {

    const [data, setData] = React.useState(10);


    return (

        <div>

            <MyComponent data={data} />

            <button onClick={() => setData(data +
1)}>Increment Data</button>

        </div>

    );

}



export default MyPage;
```

In this example, the expensiveValue is only recalculated when the data prop changes.

useCallback: This is a React Hook that memoizes a function itself. It's similar to useMemo, but instead of memoizing a value, it memoizes the function. This is useful when you pass callbacks down to child components to prevent them from re-rendering unnecessarily.

JavaScript

```javascript
import React from 'react';


function MyComponent(props) {

    console.log('Rendering MyComponent');

    return <button onClick={props.onClick}>Click Me</button>;

}



const MemoizedComponent =
React.memo(MyComponent);


function MyPage() {

    const [count, setCount] = React.useState(0);
```

```
    const handleClick = React.useCallback(() => {

        console.log('Button clicked');

    }, []);


    return (

        <div>

            <MemoizedComponent
onClick={handleClick} />

            <button onClick={() => setCount(count
+ 1)}>Increment Count</button>

        </div>

    );

}


export default MyPage;
```

In this example, the handleClick function is only re-created when its dependencies (which are empty in this case) change.

Virtualization

Virtualization is a technique that significantly improves the performance of rendering large lists or tables. Instead of rendering every single item in the list, virtualization libraries only render the items that are currently visible within the user's viewport. As the user scrolls, the library efficiently updates the rendered items, adding new ones and removing the ones that are no longer visible.

Libraries like react-window and react-virtualized are popular choices for implementing virtualization in React applications.

Here's a basic example using react-window:

JavaScript

```javascript
import React from 'react';

import { FixedSizeList as List } from
'react-window';


const Row = ({ index, style }) => {

    return <div style={style}>Row {index}</div>;

};


function MyPage() {

    return (

        <div>

            <h1>Large List</h1>

            <List

                height={150}

                itemCount={1000}

                itemSize={35}
```

```
            width={300}

      >

          {Row}

      </List>

   </div>

  );

}
```

```
export default MyPage;
```

This example renders a list of 1000 rows, but react-window only renders the rows that are currently visible within the 150px height.

Server-Side Rendering (SSR) and Static Site Generation (SSG)

We've discussed SSR and SSG earlier, but it's worth reiterating their importance for performance.

- SSR (Server-Side Rendering): Rendering the page on the server and sending the fully rendered HTML to the client. This improves SEO and perceived performance (the user sees content faster). Use getServerSideProps in Next.js.
- SSG (Static Site Generation): Generating the page at build time and serving the pre-rendered HTML. This is incredibly fast and efficient. Use getStaticProps and getStaticPaths in Next.js.

Choosing the right rendering strategy can significantly impact your application's performance.

Caching Strategies

Caching is essential for reducing server load and improving response times.

- HTTP Caching: Properly configuring HTTP caching headers allows browsers to cache assets and avoid unnecessary requests. Next.js handles some of this automatically, but you can customize it.
- Data Caching: Caching data on the server (e.g., using Redis or Memcached) can reduce the load on your database or API.
- Client-Side Caching: Techniques like storing data in localStorage or using a client-side state management library with caching features can improve performance.

Exercise

Create a Next.js page that fetches and displays data from a public API.

Implement the following optimizations:

1. Use React.memo to memoize the component that displays the data.
2. Implement client-side caching using localStorage to store the fetched data.

```JavaScript
import React, { useState, useEffect } from
'react';



const DataDisplay = React.memo(function
DataDisplay({ data }) {
```

```
    console.log('Rendering DataDisplay');

    return (

        <div>

            {data.map(item => (

                <p key={item.id}>{item.name}</p>

            ))}

        </div>

    );

});


function MyPage() {

    const [data, setData] = useState([]);

    const [loading, setLoading] = useState(true);


    useEffect(() => {

        const fetchData = async () => {

            const cachedData =
localStorage.getItem('myData');

            if (cachedData) {

                setData(JSON.parse(cachedData));

                setLoading(false);
```

```
      } else {

            const response = await
fetch('https://jsonplaceholder.typicode.com/users
'); // Replace with your API

            const newData = await
response.json();

            setData(newData);

            localStorage.setItem('myData',
JSON.stringify(newData));

            setLoading(false);

        }

    };


    fetchData();
  }, []);


  if (loading) {

    return <div>Loading...</div>;

  }


  return (

    <div>
```

```
        <h1>Data Page</h1>

        <DataDisplay data={data} />

    </div>

    );

}
```

```
export default MyPage;
```

This exercise will give you practical experience with memoization and client-side caching.

By mastering these advanced optimization techniques, you can build Next.js applications that are incredibly fast, efficient, and provide a truly exceptional user experience.

Chapter 9: Deployment and Scaling

Getting your Next.js application ready for production is a significant step. It's not just about making sure it works; it's about making sure it's reliable, performant, and can handle the load of users. Let's break down the key aspects of deployment and scaling.

9.1 Deployment Strategies (Vercel, AWS, Netlify)

Okay, let's talk about deployment strategies for your Next.js applications. This is a crucial step – taking your code from your development environment and making it accessible to users on the internet. The choice of deployment platform can significantly impact your workflow, performance, and scalability.[1] Let's break down some of the most popular options.

When it comes to deploying a Next.js application, you have several choices, each with its own set of features, advantages, and complexities. It's important to select a platform that aligns with your project's needs, budget, and technical expertise.

Vercel

Vercel is a cloud platform specifically designed for deploying and hosting web applications built with frameworks like Next.js.[2] It's developed by the creators of Next.js, which leads to a very tight integration and optimized performance.

Here's what makes Vercel stand out:

- Zero-Configuration Deployment: Vercel excels at simplifying the deployment process.[3] It automatically detects your Next.js project and handles the build and deployment setup for you.[4] You often don't need to write any configuration files. This makes it incredibly easy to get your application online quickly.

- Serverless Functions: Vercel is highly optimized for deploying Next.js API routes and serverless functions.[5] It automatically scales these functions based on traffic, so you don't have to worry about managing servers.[6]
- Edge Network: Vercel's global edge network ensures that your application is served quickly to users regardless of their location.[7] The edge network caches your application's assets and serves them from servers that are geographically close to the user, reducing latency.[8]
- Preview Deployments: Vercel's preview deployments feature is a game-changer for collaboration.[9] Every time you push a branch to your Git repository (e.g., GitHub, GitLab, Bitbucket), Vercel automatically creates a unique preview URL.[10] This allows you to test changes in a production-like environment before merging them into your main branch. This is invaluable for catching bugs and getting feedback.
- Continuous Deployment: Vercel integrates seamlessly with Git.[11] When you push updates to your main branch, Vercel automatically deploys the new version of your application.[12]

Example Workflow with Vercel:

1. You develop your Next.js application locally.
2. You connect your Git repository to Vercel.
3. Vercel automatically builds and deploys your application.[13]
4. Every time you push changes to your main branch, Vercel redeploys your application.[14]
5. Every time you push a branch, Vercel creates a preview deployment.[15]

When to Choose Vercel:

- You want the simplest and fastest deployment experience.

- You prioritize optimal performance for your Next.js application.
- You heavily use Next.js API routes and serverless functions.
- You need robust collaboration features like preview deployments.

AWS (Amazon Web Services)

Amazon Web Services (AWS) is a massive cloud computing platform that offers a vast array of services.[16] While it's very powerful and scalable, deploying Next.js applications to AWS can be more complex than using Vercel or Netlify.

Here are some of the AWS services you can use:

- AWS Amplify: AWS Amplify provides tools and services that simplify the process of building and deploying full-stack applications, including those built with Next.js.[17] It offers features like hosting, authentication, and serverless functions. Amplify can be a good option if you want to leverage other AWS services.
- AWS Elastic Beanstalk: Elastic Beanstalk is a service that makes it easy to deploy and scale web applications and services.[18] You provide your application code, and Elastic Beanstalk handles the deployment, capacity provisioning, load balancing, and health monitoring. This can be a reasonable middle ground in terms of control and ease of use.
- AWS EC2 (Elastic Compute Cloud): EC2 provides virtual servers in the cloud.[19] This gives you the most control over your deployment environment, but it also requires the most configuration and management. You're responsible for setting up the server, installing dependencies, and configuring the web server (e.g., Nginx).
- AWS S3 (Simple Storage Service) and CloudFront: If your Next.js application is mostly static (meaning it doesn't rely

heavily on server-side rendering or API routes), you can deploy it as a static site to S3 (to store the built files) and use CloudFront (AWS's Content Delivery Network) to serve the files.[20] This approach is very scalable and cost-effective for static sites.

Example: Deploying to AWS Amplify:

1. You develop your Next.js application.
2. You initialize an Amplify project.
3. You configure Amplify to build and deploy your Next.js app.
4. Amplify handles the deployment to AWS services.

When to Choose AWS:

- You need very fine-grained control over your deployment environment.
- You're already heavily invested in the AWS ecosystem and want to leverage other AWS services.
- You have complex scaling or infrastructure requirements.

Netlify

Netlify is a cloud platform that focuses on simplifying the process of building, deploying, and scaling web applications.[21] It's similar to Vercel in its ease of use but offers some distinct features.

Here are some of Netlify's key features:

- Continuous Deployment: Netlify integrates tightly with Git.[22] When you push changes to your Git repository, Netlify automatically builds and deploys the updated version of your application.[23]
- Serverless Functions: Netlify provides excellent support for serverless functions, which you can use to deploy your Next.js API routes.[24]

- Global CDN: Netlify has a global Content Delivery Network (CDN) that ensures your application's assets are served quickly to users across the globe.[25]
- Branch Deployments: Similar to Vercel's preview deployments, Netlify allows you to create unique URLs for each branch, making it easy to test and review changes.[26]

Example Workflow with Netlify:

1. You develop your Next.js application.
2. You connect your Git repository to Netlify.
3. Netlify automatically builds and deploys your application.[27]
4. Every time you push changes to your main branch, Netlify redeploys your application.[28]
5. Netlify can create deployments for branches, though the exact implementation may vary slightly from Vercel.[29]

When to Choose Netlify:

- You want a simple and efficient deployment workflow.
- You need robust support for serverless functions.
- You value features like branch deployments and a global CDN.

Key Considerations When Choosing a Platform:

- Ease of Use: How easy is it to set up and deploy your application?
- Performance: How fast will your application load for users?
- Scalability: Can the platform handle increasing traffic and data?
- Cost: What is the pricing model, and how much will it cost to host your application?
- Features: Does the platform offer features like serverless functions, CDNs, and preview deployments?
- Control: How much control do you have over the deployment environment?

Exercise:

Choose one of the deployment platforms (Vercel, AWS Amplify, or Netlify) and deploy a simple Next.js application to it.

1. Create a basic Next.js application (e.g., a simple blog or a page that displays data from an API).
2. Sign up for an account on your chosen platform.
3. Follow the platform's documentation to connect your Git repository and deploy your application.

This exercise will give you hands-on experience with the deployment process and help you understand the specific features and workflow of each platform.

9.2 Scaling Next.js Applications

Okay, let's have a detailed conversation about scaling Next.js applications. This is a crucial topic because, ideally, your application will grow in popularity, and you need to ensure it can handle the increased load without slowing down or crashing. Scaling is all about making your application resilient and performant as it faces more users and data.

Scaling, in the context of web applications, essentially means increasing your application's capacity to handle more traffic and data. It's about ensuring your application remains responsive and available, even when under heavy load. There are two main approaches to scaling:

Vertical Scaling (Scaling Up)

Vertical scaling, often called "scaling up," involves increasing the resources of a single server.

This means upgrading the server's hardware, such as:

- CPU: Adding more or faster processors.

- RAM: Increasing the amount of memory.
- Storage: Using faster or larger storage devices (e.g., SSDs).

Think of it like upgrading your computer. If your computer is running slowly, you might upgrade the processor or add more RAM to make it faster.

Advantages of Vertical Scaling:

- Simpler to Implement: It's often easier to upgrade a single server than to set up a distributed system.
- Less Complex Architecture: You don't have to deal with the complexities of load balancing, distributed data, and network communication between multiple servers.

Disadvantages of Vertical Scaling:

- Limitations: There's a finite limit to how much you can increase the resources of a single server. You'll eventually hit a hardware bottleneck.
- Single Point of Failure: If the single server goes down, your entire application goes down.
- Downtime: Upgrading a server may require downtime.

When Vertical Scaling Might Be Suitable:

- For small to medium-sized applications with moderate traffic.
- When you need a quick and simple way to increase capacity.
- When your application's bottleneck is clearly CPU, RAM, or storage on a single server.

Horizontal Scaling (Scaling Out)

Horizontal scaling, also called "scaling out," involves adding more servers to your infrastructure. Instead of making one server more powerful, you distribute the load across multiple servers.

Think of it like adding more checkout lines at a grocery store. If there are long lines, you open more lines to serve customers faster.

Advantages of Horizontal Scaling:

- Scalability: You can theoretically scale indefinitely by adding more servers.
- High Availability: If one server goes down, the other servers can continue to serve traffic.
- Fault Tolerance: Horizontal scaling provides redundancy and fault tolerance.

Disadvantages of Horizontal Scaling:

- Complexity: Setting up and managing a distributed system is more complex than managing a single server.
- Load Balancing: You need a load balancer to distribute traffic across the servers.
- Data Management: You need to consider how to share data between the servers (e.g., using a distributed database or caching system).
- Increased Costs: Running multiple servers is generally more expensive than running a single server.

When Horizontal Scaling Is Essential:

- For large-scale applications with high traffic volumes.
- When you need high availability and fault tolerance.
- When you anticipate significant growth in your application's user base.

Scaling Strategies for Next.js Applications

Now, let's discuss how these scaling principles apply specifically to Next.js applications:

- Serverless Functions (for API Routes): If you're using Next.js API routes, you're already leveraging a form of horizontal scaling. Platforms like Vercel and Netlify automatically scale your serverless functions. They spin up more function instances to handle increased requests. You generally don't have to configure this manually, which is a significant advantage.

- Load Balancing: If you're deploying your Next.js application to your own servers (e.g., on AWS EC2), you'll likely need a load balancer. A load balancer distributes incoming traffic across multiple server instances. Common load balancers include:
  - Nginx: A popular open-source web server and reverse proxy that can also act as a load balancer.
  - HAProxy: Another open-source load balancer.
  - AWS Elastic Load Balancing: A service provided by AWS.

- Caching: Caching is crucial for scaling. By reducing the number of requests that your server has to handle, you can significantly improve performance and scalability.
  - HTTP Caching: Configure HTTP caching headers (e.g., Cache-Control) to instruct browsers and CDNs to cache assets. Next.js handles some of this automatically.
  - CDN (Content Delivery Network): Use a CDN to serve static assets (like images, CSS, and JavaScript) from servers closer to the user. This reduces latency. Services like Cloudflare, AWS CloudFront, and Netlify's CDN are excellent options.
  - Data Caching: If your application fetches data from a database or API, caching that data can drastically reduce the load on your data source. You can use in-memory caches (e.g., Redis or Memcached) or implement caching within your application.

- Database Scaling: If your Next.js application relies on a database, you'll need to scale your database as well. This is a complex topic in itself, but here are some common strategies:

- o Vertical Scaling: Upgrading your database server's hardware.
- o Read Replicas: Creating multiple copies of your database to handle read requests.
- o Sharding: Partitioning your database across multiple servers.
- Server-Side Rendering (SSR) vs. Static Site Generation (SSG): The choice between SSR and SSG can impact scalability.
  - o SSG: Static Site Generation is generally more scalable because the pages are pre-rendered at build time. The server simply serves the static HTML files, which is very efficient.
  - o SSR: Server-Side Rendering can be less scalable because the server has to render the page for each request. However, you can optimize SSR with caching.

Example: Scaling a Next.js Application on AWS

Let's say you're deploying a Next.js application to AWS and you're experiencing high traffic. Here's a possible scaling strategy:

1. EC2 Instances: Deploy your Next.js application to multiple EC2 instances.
2. Elastic Load Balancing: Use AWS Elastic Load Balancing to distribute incoming traffic across the EC2 instances.
3. Auto Scaling: Configure AWS Auto Scaling to automatically add or remove EC2 instances based on traffic demand.
4. CloudFront: Use AWS CloudFront to cache and serve static assets.

RDS (Relational Database Service)

Use AWS RDS for your database and scale it using read replicas or other RDS scaling features.

Exercise

Choose a hypothetical Next.js application (e.g., a blog, an e-commerce site, a social media platform) and describe a scaling strategy for it.

1. Describe the application's architecture (e.g., what data sources it uses, how it handles user requests).
2. Identify potential scaling bottlenecks.
3. Outline the scaling strategies you would use (vertical or horizontal scaling, load balancing, caching, etc.).
4. Explain how your scaling strategy would address the identified bottlenecks.

This exercise will help you think through the process of designing a scalable Next.js application.

9.3 Monitoring and Maintaining Production Applications

Okay, let's talk about monitoring and maintaining your Next.js applications in production. This is a crucial phase of the application lifecycle, and it's where you ensure your application remains healthy, performs well, and provides a reliable experience for your users.

Think of it like owning a car. You don't just drive it until it breaks down, right? You perform regular maintenance, check the engine, monitor the fuel, and address any issues promptly. The same proactive approach is essential for your production applications.

Here's a breakdown of the key aspects of monitoring and maintenance:

Performance Monitoring

Performance monitoring involves tracking key metrics to understand how your application is performing in the real world. This helps you identify bottlenecks, detect slowdowns, and ensure your application is responsive.

- Key Performance Indicators (KPIs): Define the metrics that are most important for your application. Common KPIs include:
  - Page Load Time: How long it takes for a page to fully load.
  - Time to First Byte (TTFB): How long it takes for the browser to receive the first byte of data from the server.
  - Response Time: How long it takes for API requests to complete.
  - Error Rate: The percentage of requests that result in errors.
  - CPU and Memory Usage: The amount of server resources your application is consuming.
  - Database Query Time: How long it takes for database queries to execute.
- Tools and Techniques:
  - Browser Developer Tools: As we discussed earlier, browser developer tools (especially the Network and Performance tabs) are invaluable for analyzing client-side performance. You can use them to inspect requests, identify slow-loading resources, and profile JavaScript execution.
  - Lighthouse: Chrome's Lighthouse tool provides automated audits for performance, accessibility, SEO, and other metrics. It gives you a score and provides recommendations for improvement.

- Real User Monitoring (RUM): RUM involves collecting performance data from real users in their browsers. This gives you insights into how your application performs under various conditions (network speeds, devices, etc.). RUM tools can track metrics like page load times, first input delay, and JavaScript errors.
- Server Monitoring Tools: Tools like Prometheus, Grafana, and Datadog can help you monitor server-side performance, including CPU usage, memory usage, and response times.
- Application Performance Monitoring (APM): APM tools (like New Relic, Datadog, and Sentry) provide detailed insights into your application's performance, including request tracing, database query analysis, and error tracking.

Example: Setting up basic performance monitoring

Let's say you want to track page load times. You could use browser's PerformanceObserver API to collect this data and send it to your server:

```
JavaScript

// In a component or a global script


if (window.PerformanceObserver) {

    const observer = new
PerformanceObserver((entryList) => {

        entryList.getEntries().forEach((entry) =>
{
```

```
        if (entry.entryType === 'navigation')
{

            const pageLoadTime =
entry.loadEventEnd - entry.startTime;

            console.log(`Page load time:
${pageLoadTime}ms`);

            // Send this data to your server

            // fetch('/api/performance', {

            //     method: 'POST',

            //     body: JSON.stringify({
pageLoadTime }),

            //     headers: { 'Content-Type':
'application/json' },

            // });

        }

    });

  });



  observer.observe({ type: 'navigation',
buffered: true });

}
```

PerformanceObserver: This API allows you to observe performance-related events in the browser.

We observe navigation entries to get page load timing information.

entry.loadEventEnd - entry.startTime calculates the time from the start of the navigation to the load event.

The commented-out fetch call shows how you could send this data to your server for analysis.

Error Tracking

Error tracking is essential for identifying and addressing issues that can impact your application's stability and user experience.

- Logging: Implement comprehensive logging to record events and errors in your application. Use different log levels (e.g., info, warn, error) to categorize log messages.
- Error Tracking Services: Services like Sentry, Bugsnag, and Rollbar help you capture and analyze JavaScript errors in the browser and server-side errors. These services provide detailed information about errors, including stack traces, user context, and browser information.

Example: Using Sentry for error tracking

JavaScript

```
// Install Sentry: npm install @sentry/react
@sentry/tracing
```

```
import * as Sentry from "@sentry/react";

import { BrowserTracing } from "@sentry/tracing";
```

```
Sentry.init({

  dsn: "YOUR_SENTRY_DSN", // Replace with your
Sentry DSN

  integrations: [new BrowserTracing()],

  tracesSampleRate: 1.0, // Capture 100% of
transactions for performance monitoring

});


function MyApp({ Component, pageProps }) {

  return (

    <Sentry.ErrorBoundary fallback={<p>An error
occurred</p>} showDialog>

      <Component {...pageProps} />

    </Sentry.ErrorBoundary>

  );

}


export default MyApp;
```

- Sentry.init(): Initializes Sentry with your DSN (Data Source Name).
- BrowserTracing: Enables performance monitoring of browser events.
- tracesSampleRate: Controls the percentage of transactions that Sentry will track.

- Sentry.ErrorBoundary: A React component that catches errors in its child components and allows you to display a fallback UI.

Logging

Effective logging provides a record of events and actions within your application.

This is invaluable for:

- Debugging: Understanding what happened when an error occurs.
- Auditing: Tracking user activity and security events.
- Monitoring: Identifying patterns and trends in application behavior.
- Logging Levels: Use different logging levels to categorize messages:
    - debug: Detailed information for developers.
    - info: General information about application events.
    - warn: Potential issues that may not be errors.
    - error: Errors that need attention.
    - fatal: Critical errors that cause application failure.
- Structured Logging: Consider using structured logging formats (like JSON) to make it easier to search and analyze log data.
- Logging Libraries: Libraries like Winston and Bunyan can help you implement robust logging in Node.js applications.

Security Updates

Keeping your application secure is an ongoing responsibility.

- Dependency Updates: Regularly update your Next.js, React, and all other dependencies to the latest versions. Security vulnerabilities are often discovered and patched in newer versions.

- Security Audits: Use tools like npm audit or yarn audit to identify known vulnerabilities in your dependencies.
- Stay Informed: Keep up-to-date with security best practices and news about vulnerabilities that might affect your application.

Regular Backups

Back up your data and application code regularly to prevent data loss in case of hardware failure, software errors, or security breaches.

- Database Backups: Implement a robust database backup strategy.
- Code Repository Backups: Use a version control system (like Git) and consider having backups of your code repository.

Deployment Automation

Automating your deployment process can significantly reduce errors and improve efficiency.

- Continuous Integration/Continuous Deployment (CI/CD): Use CI/CD pipelines to automate the process of building, testing, and deploying your application.
- Infrastructure as Code (IaC): Use tools like Terraform or CloudFormation to manage your infrastructure as code, making it easier to reproduce and manage.

Exercise

1. Choose a simple Next.js application you've created.
2. Set up basic logging in your API routes. Log information about incoming requests, successful responses, and any errors that occur.

3. Install Sentry and configure it to track JavaScript errors in your application.
4. Use npm audit or yarn audit to check for vulnerabilities in your dependencies.

This exercise will give you practical experience in setting up logging and error tracking, which are essential for maintaining production applications.

Chapter 10: Testing and Debugging

Testing and debugging are integral parts of the software development lifecycle. They help ensure the quality, reliability, and maintainability of your Next.js applications. Let's explore different testing types and debugging techniques.

10.1 Unit, Integration, and End-to-End Testing

Okay, let's have a really detailed discussion about unit, integration, and end-to-end testing. This is a fundamental part of software development, and especially important when working with frameworks like Next.js where you have both front-end and back-end code intertwined.

Testing is not just about finding bugs; it's about building confidence in your code.[1] It's about creating a safety net that allows you to make changes without fear of breaking things. It's about ensuring your application behaves as expected, consistently.

Let's break down the different types of testing:

Unit Testing

Unit testing is the most granular level of testing.[2] It focuses on testing individual units of code in isolation.[3] A "unit" can be a function, a class, a module, or even a single component in React. The goal is to verify that each unit performs its specific task correctly.

Think of it like testing the individual parts of a car engine. You'd test the spark plugs, the pistons, and the fuel injectors separately to make sure each one is working as designed.

Key Characteristics of Unit Tests:

- Isolation: Unit tests should isolate the unit being tested from its dependencies.[4] This often involves using mocks or stubs to simulate the behavior of other parts of the system.[5]
- Speed: Unit tests should be fast to execute.[6] You'll often run them frequently, so speed is crucial.
- Focus: They focus on the logic within the unit itself, not how it interacts with other units.[7]

Tools for Unit Testing:

- Jest: A popular JavaScript testing framework, especially well-suited for React applications.[8] It provides a rich set of features, including mocking, assertions, and test runners.
- Mocha: Another flexible JavaScript testing framework that allows you to choose your assertion library and test runner.[9]
- Chai: An assertion library that can be used with Mocha or other testing frameworks.[10]
- React Testing Library: A library specifically designed for testing React components. It encourages testing from the user's perspective, focusing on how components render and behave in response to user interactions.

Example: Unit Testing a React Component

Let's say you have a simple React component that displays a greeting:

```javascript
JavaScript


// components/Greeting.js

import React from 'react';



function Greeting({ name }) {
```

```
    return (

        <h1>Hello, {name}!</h1>

    );

}


export default Greeting;
```

Here's how you might write a unit test for this component using Jest and React Testing Library:

JavaScript

```javascript
// components/Greeting.test.js

import React from 'react';

import { render, screen } from
'@testing-library/react';

import Greeting from './Greeting';


describe('Greeting Component', () => {

    it('renders the correct greeting', () => {

        render(<Greeting name="World" />);

        const greetingElement =
screen.getByText('Hello, World!');


expect(greetingElement).toBeInTheDocument();
```

```
  });



  it('renders a different greeting when the
name prop changes', () => {

      const { rerender } = render(<Greeting
name="User" />);

      const greetingElement =
screen.getByText('Hello, User!');


expect(greetingElement).toBeInTheDocument();



      rerender(<Greeting name="Test User" />);

      const newGreetingElement =
screen.getByText('Hello, Test User!');


expect(newGreetingElement).toBeInTheDocument();

  });

});
```

Explanation:

- describe('Greeting Component', () => { ... });: This groups related tests together.
- it('renders the correct greeting', () => { ... });: This defines a single test case.
- render(<Greeting name="World" />);: This renders the Greeting component with the name prop set to "World".

- screen.getByText('Hello, World!'): This uses React Testing Library's screen object to find an element on the page that contains the text "Hello, World!".
- expect(greetingElement).toBeInTheDocument();: This is an assertion using Jest's expect function. It checks that the greetingElement was found in the rendered output.
- rerender(<Greeting name="Test User" />);: This function is returned by render and allows you to update the props and re-render the component.

Benefits of Unit Testing:

- Early Bug Detection: Unit tests help you find bugs early in the development process, when they're easier and cheaper to fix.[11]
- Improved Code Quality: Writing unit tests encourages you to write cleaner, more modular, and more testable code.[12]
- Facilitates Refactoring: When you refactor your code (change its internal structure without changing its external behavior), unit tests act as a safety net, ensuring that you haven't broken anything.[13]
- Documentation: Unit tests can serve as a form of documentation, showing how individual units of code are supposed to be used.[14]

Integration Testing

Integration testing focuses on testing how different units of code work together.[15] It verifies that the interactions between components, modules, or services are correct.

Think of it as testing how the engine, transmission, and wheels of a car work together. You've already tested each part individually (unit testing), but now you want to make sure they function correctly as a system.

Key Characteristics of Integration Tests:

- Interaction: Integration tests emphasize the communication and data flow between different parts of the application.[16]
- Scope: They cover a broader scope than unit tests, testing the integration of multiple units.[17]
- Dependencies: Integration tests may involve real dependencies, such as databases or APIs, although mocks and stubs can still be used to control external behavior.[18]

Tools for Integration Testing:

- Jest: Can be used for integration testing, especially for testing React components that interact with each other.[19]
- React Testing Library: Also excellent for integration testing React components, as it focuses on testing user interactions and component behavior.

Example: Integration Testing React Components

Let's say you have two React components: a SearchBar that allows users to enter a search term, and a SearchResults component that displays the results.

JavaScript

```
// components/SearchBar.js

import React, { useState } from 'react';



function SearchBar({ onSearch }) {

    const [searchTerm, setSearchTerm] =
useState('');
```

```javascript
    const handleInputChange = (event) => {

        setSearchTerm(event.target.value);

    };


    const handleSearchClick = () => {

        onSearch(searchTerm);

    };


    return (

        <div>

            <input type="text" value={searchTerm}
onChange={handleInputChange} />

            <button
onClick={handleSearchClick}>Search</button>

        </div>

    );

}


export default SearchBar;


// components/SearchResults.js
```

```javascript
import React from 'react';


function SearchResults({ results }) {

    return (

        <ul>

            {results.map(result => (

                <li
key={result.id}>{result.title}</li>

            ))}

        </ul>

    );

}


export default SearchResults;
```

Here's an integration test using React Testing Library:

JavaScript

```javascript
// components/SearchBar.test.js

import React from 'react';

import { render, screen, fireEvent } from
'@testing-library/react';

import SearchBar from './SearchBar';
```

```
describe('SearchBar Component', () => {

    it('calls the onSearch callback with the
search term when the button is clicked', () => {

        const mockOnSearch = jest.fn(); // Create
a mock function

        render(<SearchBar onSearch={mockOnSearch}
/>);


        const inputElement =
screen.getByRole('textbox');

        const buttonElement =
screen.getByRole('button', { name: 'Search' });


        fireEvent.change(inputElement, { target:
{ value: 'test' } }); // Simulate typing in the
input

        fireEvent.click(buttonElement); //
Simulate clicking the button


expect(mockOnSearch).toHaveBeenCalledWith('test')
; // Assert that the callback was called with the
correct argument

    });
```

```
});
```

Explanation:

- const mockOnSearch = jest.fn();: This creates a mock function using Jest's jest.fn(). A mock function is a function that you can use to simulate the behavior of a real function.[20]
- render(<SearchBar onSearch={mockOnSearch} />);: This renders the SearchBar component, passing the mock function as the onSearch prop.
- screen.getByRole('textbox'): This finds the input element using React Testing Library's screen.getByRole(), which is a good practice for accessibility.
- fireEvent.change(inputElement, { target: { value: 'test' } });: This simulates typing "test" into the input element.
- fireEvent.click(buttonElement);: This simulates clicking the button.
- expect(mockOnSearch).toHaveBeenCalledWith('test');: This asserts that the mockOnSearch function was called with the argument "test".

Benefits of Integration Testing:

- Verifies Component Interactions: Integration tests ensure that your components work together correctly, which is crucial for building complex applications.[21]
- Finds Interface Issues: They can uncover issues related to how components pass data or communicate with each other.
- Builds Confidence in Larger Systems: Integration tests give you more confidence that your application's different parts are working as expected.[22]

End-to-End (E2E) Testing

End-to-end (E2E) testing is the highest level of testing. It tests the entire application flow from start to finish, simulating real user behavior. E2E tests verify that the application works correctly as a whole, from the user interface to the database.[23]

Think of it like testing a car by taking it for a test drive. You'd check everything from starting the engine to braking and steering.

Key Characteristics of E2E Tests:

- Full Application Flow: E2E tests cover complete user scenarios.[24]
- Real-World Simulation: They try to mimic how users actually interact with the application.
- Environment: E2E tests are often performed in a test environment that closely resembles the production environment.[25]

Tools for End-to-End Testing:

- Cypress: A popular E2E testing framework that runs tests directly in the browser.[26] It provides features like time travel debugging and automatic waiting.[27]
- Playwright: A relatively new E2E testing framework developed by Microsoft.[28] It supports multiple browsers and offers powerful features like auto-waiting and network request mocking.
- Selenium: A widely used E2E testing framework that can automate web browsers.[29]

Example: End-to-End Testing a Login Flow (Conceptual)

Let's say you have a login flow in your Next.js application.

Here's a conceptual example of an E2E test using Cypress:

JavaScript

```javascript
// cypress/integration/login.spec.js


describe('Login Flow', () => {

    it('allows a user to log in successfully', ()
=> {

        cy.visit('/login'); // Visit the login
page

cy.get('input[name="email"]').type('test@example.
com'); // Type the email


cy.get('input[name="password"]').type('password')
; // Type the password

        cy.get('button[type="submit"]').click();
// Click the submit button

        cy.url().should('include', '/dashboard');
// Assert that the URL changes to the dashboard

        cy.get('h1').should('contain',
'Dashboard'); // Assert that the dashboard
heading is displayed

    });
```

```
    it('displays an error message for invalid
credentials', () => {

        cy.visit('/login');


cy.get('input[name="email"]').type('invalid@examp
le.com');


cy.get('input[name="password"]').type('wrongpassw
ord');

        cy.get('button[type="submit"]').click();


cy.get('.error-message').should('contain',
'Invalid credentials'); // Assert that the error
message is displayed

    });

});
```

Explanation:

- cy.visit('/login');: This tells Cypress to visit the login page.
- cy.get('input[name="email"]').type('test@example.com');: This finds the input element with the name "email" and types the email address into it.
- cy.get('button[type="submit"]').click();: This finds the button with the type "submit" and clicks it.
- cy.url().should('include', '/dashboard');: This asserts that the current URL includes "/dashboard" after the login button is clicked.
- cy.get('h1').should('contain', 'Dashboard');: This asserts that an <h1> element on the page contains the text "Dashboard".

- cy.get('.error-message').should('contain', 'Invalid credentials');: This asserts that an element with the class "error-message" contains the text "Invalid credentials".

Benefits of End-to-End Testing:

- Verifies Entire Application Flow: E2E tests ensure that the application works correctly from the user's perspective, covering all layers of the system.[30]
- Finds Integration Issues: They can uncover issues that may not be apparent in unit or integration tests, such as problems with routing, data flow, or third-party integrations.
- Builds Confidence in Release: Successful E2E tests give you a high level of confidence that your application is ready for release.

In Summary

- Unit Tests: Test individual units of code (small, fast, isolated).[31]
- Integration Tests: Test how different units work together (medium scope, focus on interactions).[32]
- End-to-End Tests: Test the entire application flow (large scope, simulates user behavior).[33]

A well-rounded testing strategy typically involves a combination of all three types of testing. Unit tests provide a strong foundation, integration tests verify component interactions, and E2E tests ensure the application works correctly as a whole.

10.2 Debugging Next.js Applications

Okay, let's have a really thorough conversation about debugging Next.js applications. This is a skill that every developer needs to hone, because no matter how careful you are, you're going to run into bugs. Debugging is the process of identifying, locating, and fixing errors in your code, and it's a critical part of the development workflow.

Debugging can sometimes feel like detective work, but with the right tools and techniques, you can become much more efficient at it.

Understanding the Challenges of Debugging Next.js

Next.js applications can present some unique debugging challenges because they involve both client-side (browser) and server-side code. You have to consider where the error is occurring to choose the appropriate debugging approach.

Browser Developer Tools

The browser's developer tools are your primary ally for debugging client-side code (the code that runs in the user's browser). All modern browsers (Chrome, Firefox, Safari, Edge) provide these tools, and they are incredibly powerful.

Here are the key parts of the developer tools that you'll use most often:

Console

The console is where you can log messages, warnings, and errors. It's also where you can execute JavaScript code directly in the browser's context.

- console.log(): The most basic way to print values and messages to the console.
- console.warn(): Prints a warning message.
- console.error(): Prints an error message.
- console.table(): Prints data in a table format, which can be useful for inspecting arrays and objects.

Elements

This tab allows you to inspect the HTML and CSS of the page. You can see the structure of the DOM (Document Object Model) and how styles are applied to elements. This is useful for debugging layout issues and CSS problems.

Network

The Network tab shows you all the network requests that the browser makes (e.g., fetching data from an API, loading images). You can see the status of each request, how long it took, the headers, and the response data. This is essential for debugging API calls and network-related issues.

Sources (or Debugger)

This tab is where you can set breakpoints in your JavaScript code and step through it line by line. Breakpoints pause the execution of your code, allowing you to inspect variables and understand the program's state.

Application

This tab provides tools for inspecting and managing various application resources, such as cookies, local storage, and session storage. This is useful for debugging session management and data persistence issues.

Performance

This tab allows you to record a performance profile of your page. You can see how long it takes for the browser to execute

JavaScript, render the page, and perform other tasks. This is helpful for identifying performance bottlenecks.

Example: Using the Chrome Debugger

Let's say you have a function that's not working as expected:

JavaScript

```javascript
function calculateTotal(items) {

    let total = 0;

    for (let i = 0; i <= items.length; i++)
{ // Intentional error: i <= items.length

        total += items[i].price;

    }

    return total;

}

const cartItems = [

    { price: 10 },

    { price: 20 },

    { price: 30 },

];
```

```
const total = calculateTotal(cartItems);

console.log('Total:', total);
```

Here's how you might debug this using Chrome:

1. Open Chrome Developer Tools (usually by pressing F12).
2. Go to the "Sources" tab.
3. Find the file containing this code.
4. Click in the gutter (the area to the left of the line numbers) to set a breakpoint on the first line of the calculateTotal function.
5. Reload the page. Chrome will pause execution at your breakpoint.
6. Use the "Step Over" button (or press F10) to execute the code line by line.
7. Hover your mouse over variables to inspect their values.
8. You'll quickly see that the loop condition i <= items.length is causing an error because it tries to access items[items.length], which is out of bounds.
9. Fix the code: for (let i = 0; i < items.length; i++) { ... }

Next.js Devtools (Experimental)

Next.js provides an experimental devtools extension that offers insights into Next.js-specific features. It can help you understand how data fetching is working, how routing is handled, and other Next.js internals.

To use it, you'll typically need to install it as a Chrome extension (search the Chrome Web Store). Once installed, it will appear as a tab in your developer tools when you're working with a Next.js application.

Example: Using Next.js Devtools

If you're having trouble with data fetching, the Next.js Devtools might show you:

- Which data fetching methods are being called (getServerSideProps, getStaticProps, etc.).
- How long each data fetching operation is taking.
- Whether data is being cached or fetched from the server.

Debugging in VS Code

If you're using Visual Studio Code (VS Code) as your code editor, you can configure it to debug your Next.js application directly. This allows you to set breakpoints, step through code, and inspect variables within your editor, which can be very convenient.

VS Code has debugging configurations for both Node.js (for server-side code) and Chrome (for client-side code).

Example: Debugging a Next.js API Route in VS Code

1. In VS Code, go to the "Run and Debug" view (Ctrl+Shift+D or Cmd+Shift+D).
2. Click the gear icon to create a launch.json file.
3. Choose "Node.js: Launch Program" as the environment.
4. Modify the launch.json file to point to your API route file:

JSON

```json
{

    "version": "0.2.0",

    "configurations": [
```

```
{

    "type": "node",

    "request": "launch",

    "name": "Launch API Route",

    "program":
"${workspaceFolder}/pages/api/my-api-route.js" //
Replace with your API route file

    }

  ]

}
```

Set breakpoints in your API route code.

Press F5 to start debugging. VS Code will execute your API route, and you can step through the code and inspect variables.

General Debugging Tips

- Read Error Messages Carefully: Error messages often provide valuable clues about the source of the problem. Pay attention to the line numbers and the type of error.
- Isolate the Problem: Try to narrow down the source of the bug. Simplify your code, remove unnecessary elements, and test smaller parts of the application.
- Use Version Control: Use Git (or another version control system) to track your changes. If you introduce a bug, you can easily revert to a previous working version.

- Rubber Duck Debugging: Explain your code to someone (or even an inanimate object like a rubber duck). The act of explaining can often help you identify errors in your logic.
- Learn to Use the Profiler: The React Profiler (in React DevTools) helps you identify performance bottlenecks in your components. It shows you how long each component takes to render and why components re-render.
- Don't Guess, Investigate: Instead of making random changes and hoping they fix the problem, use your debugging tools to systematically investigate the cause of the bug.

Debugging is a skill that improves with practice. The more you use your debugging tools and apply these techniques, the more efficient and effective you'll become at finding and fixing errors in your Next.js applications.

10.3 Using Debugging Tools and Techniques

Okay, let's have a really practical discussion about using debugging tools and techniques. We've talked about the tools themselves, but now it's time to get into the specific strategies and methods that will make you a more effective debugger. Debugging isn't just about knowing the tools; it's about having a systematic approach to problem-solving.

Debugging can be frustrating, but if you approach it methodically, you'll find that you can solve even the most challenging problems.

Here are some key debugging tools and techniques, along with detailed explanations and examples:

console.log(), console.warn(), and console.error()

These are the workhorses of JavaScript debugging. They allow you to print messages, warnings, and errors to the browser's console. While seemingly simple, they are incredibly versatile.

console.log(): Use this for general-purpose logging of values, messages, and any information you want to inspect.

JavaScript

```javascript
function myFunction(value) {

    console.log('Function called with value:',
value);

    const result = value * 2;

    console.log('Result:', result);

    return result;

}



myFunction(5);
```

console.warn(): Use this to indicate something unexpected or potentially problematic, but not necessarily an error that will crash the application.

JavaScript

```javascript
function processData(data) {
```

```
if (!data) {

    console.warn('processData called with
null or undefined data');

    return; // Early return to prevent errors

}

// ... process data

}
```

```
processData(null);
```

console.error(): Use this to log actual errors that indicate something has gone wrong and needs to be fixed.

JavaScript

```
try {

    const result = JSON.parse(invalidJsonString);

} catch (error) {

    console.error('Error parsing JSON:', error);

}
```

console.table(): This is a lesser-known but very useful method for printing arrays of objects in a tabular format, making them easier to read.

JavaScript

```
const users = [

    { id: 1, name: 'Alice', age: 30 },

    { id: 2, name: 'Bob', age: 25 },

    { id: 3, name: 'Charlie', age: 35 },

];

console.table(users);
```

Using Breakpoints in the Browser's Debugger

This is a core skill for any JavaScript developer. Breakpoints allow you to pause the execution of your code at a specific line and inspect the state of your application.

Here's how to use breakpoints in Chrome (the process is similar in other browsers):

1. Open Chrome Developer Tools (usually by pressing F12).
2. Go to the "Sources" tab.
3. Find the JavaScript file containing the code you want to debug.
4. Click in the gutter (the area to the left of the line numbers) to set a breakpoint. A red dot will appear.
5. Reload the page or trigger the code that you're debugging. Chrome will pause execution at your breakpoint.

Once execution is paused, you can:

-   Inspect Variables: Hover your mouse over variables to see their current values.
-   Step Through Code: Use the "Step Over" (F10), "Step Into" (F11), and "Step Out" (Shift+F11) buttons to control the execution flow.
-   Watch Expressions: Add expressions to the "Watch" panel to monitor their values as the code executes.

- View the Call Stack: See the sequence of function calls that led to the current point in the code.

Example:

JavaScript

```
function calculateArea(width, height) {

    const area = width * height;

    return area;

}



function displayArea(width, height) {

    const area = calculateArea(width, height);

    console.log('Area:', area);

}



displayArea(10, 5); // Set a breakpoint here
```

If you set a breakpoint in calculateArea, you can step through the calculation and see the values of width, height, and area at each step.

The debugger; Statement

You can also insert the debugger; statement directly into your code to create a breakpoint:

JavaScript

```
function myFunction(value) {

    debugger; // Execution will pause here

    const result = value * 2;

    return result;

}



myFunction(5);
```

When the browser encounters the debugger; statement, it will pause execution (if the developer tools are open).

Using the React DevTools

The React DevTools browser extension is essential for debugging React applications.

It allows you to:

- Inspect the Component Tree: See the hierarchy of your React components.
- View Props and State: Inspect the current props and state of each component.
- Track Updates: See when and why components are re-rendering.
- Profile Performance: Identify performance bottlenecks by measuring how long it takes components to render.

Example:

If you're having trouble with a component not updating correctly, you can use React DevTools to:

- Select the component in the component tree.

- See if the props or state that should be causing an update are actually changing.
- Use the Profiler to see if the component is re-rendering more often than necessary.

Logging on the Server (for Next.js API Routes)

When debugging Next.js API routes (server-side code), you'll need to log information on the server. You can use Node.js's built-in console.log(), console.warn(), and console.error(), but for more robust logging, consider using a logging library like Winston or Bunyan.

Example:

JavaScript

```javascript
// pages/api/my-api-route.js


export default function handler(req, res) {

    console.log('Received request to
/api/my-api-route');

    try {

        // ... your API logic

        res.status(200).json({ data: 'Success'
});

    } catch (error) {

        console.error('Error in
/api/my-api-route:', error);
```

```
    res.status(500).json({ error: 'Internal
Server Error' });

  }

}
```

Debugging Techniques

- Read Error Messages Carefully: This seems obvious, but often the error message contains the exact clue you need. Pay attention to the line numbers, the type of error, and any other details.
- Isolate the Problem: Try to narrow down the source of the bug. Simplify your code, remove unnecessary parts, and test smaller sections in isolation.
- Reproduce the Bug Consistently: If you can't reliably reproduce the bug, it will be much harder to fix. Identify the exact steps that lead to the error.
- Rubber Duck Debugging: Explain your code, line by line, to someone (or even a rubber duck). This forces you to think through the logic and often helps you spot errors.
- Use Version Control (Git): If you're using Git (and you should be!), use it to your advantage. If you introduce a bug, you can easily revert to a previous working version using git revert or git checkout.
- Don't Guess, Investigate: Instead of randomly changing code and hoping it works, use your debugging tools to gather information and form a hypothesis about the cause of the bug. Then, test your hypothesis.
- Learn to Use the Profiler: The React Profiler (in React DevTools) is crucial for identifying performance bottlenecks. It shows you which components are re-rendering and how long each render takes.

Debugging is a skill that gets better with practice. The more you use these tools and techniques, the more efficient and confident you'll become at finding and fixing bugs in your Next.js applications.

Chapter 11: Next.js Ecosystem and Future Trends

Next.js isn't just a framework; it's a vibrant ecosystem with a lot of supporting tools and a community that's constantly pushing the boundaries of what's possible. It's also evolving rapidly, so staying up-to-date with emerging trends is crucial.

11.1 Exploring Popular Next.js Libraries and Tools

Okay, let's talk about the Next.js ecosystem. It's not just the core framework itself; it's also the collection of libraries and tools that extend its functionality and make our lives as developers easier.[1] Think of it like this: Next.js provides the foundation for building a house, and these libraries are like the specialized tools and materials that help you finish the job – plumbing, electrical wiring, etc.

It's important to be aware of these tools because they can significantly streamline your workflow and allow you to build more complex and robust applications. Let's explore some of the most popular and useful ones.

next-auth

next-auth is a powerful library that simplifies authentication in Next.js applications. Authentication, as you know, is the process of verifying who a user is.[2] It's a critical part of most web applications, but it can be complex to implement correctly.

next-auth **handles a lot of the heavy lifting for you, including:**

- Supporting various authentication providers: It allows you to authenticate users using traditional username/password combinations, social logins (like Google, Facebook, GitHub), and even passwordless authentication.[3]

- Session management: It manages user sessions, so users don't have to log in on every page request.[4]
- Security best practices: It implements security best practices to protect your application from common authentication vulnerabilities.[5]

Why is next-auth **helpful?**

- Saves time and effort: You don't have to write a lot of code from scratch to handle authentication.
- Improves security: It helps you implement authentication securely, reducing the risk of vulnerabilities.[6]
- Provides a consistent API: It provides a consistent API for working with different authentication providers.

Example:

Here's a simplified example of how you might use next-auth to add Google login to your Next.js application:

```
JavaScript
```

```
// pages/api/auth/[...nextauth].js (This is a
special API route for next-auth)



import NextAuth from 'next-auth';

import GoogleProvider from
'next-auth/providers/google';



export default NextAuth({
```

```
providers: [

    GoogleProvider({

        clientId:
process.env.GOOGLE_CLIENT_ID,

        clientSecret:
process.env.GOOGLE_CLIENT_SECRET,

    }),

  ],

  secret: process.env.NEXTAUTH_SECRET,

  callbacks: {

      async session({ session, token, user }) {

          // Send properties to the client,
like an access_token from a provider.

          session.accessToken =
token.accessToken;

          return session;

      },

  },

});
```

- This code sets up an API route that handles authentication.
- It uses the GoogleProvider to enable Google login.
- You'll need to obtain GOOGLE_CLIENT_ID and GOOGLE_CLIENT_SECRET from the Google Cloud Console.

- NEXTAUTH_SECRET is a random string used to encrypt tokens; store it securely.
- The callbacks section allows you to customize how the session data is handled.

To use the session information in your components, you can use the useSession hook:

JavaScript

```javascript
import { useSession, signIn, signOut } from
'next-auth/react';


function MyComponent() {

    const { data: session } = useSession();


    if (session) {

        return (

            <div>

                <p>Welcome,
{session.user.email}!</p>

                <button onClick={() =>
signOut()}>Sign out</button>

            </div>

        );

    }
```

```
  return (

    <div>

      <p>You are not signed in.</p>

      <button onClick={() => signIn()}>Sign
in</button>

    </div>

  );

}
```

react-query

react-query is a library that helps you manage data fetching, caching, and updating in your React components. Fetching data from APIs is a common task in web development, and react-query makes it much easier and more efficient.

Why is react-query helpful?

- Simplified data fetching: It handles things like caching, retries, and background updates for you.
- Improved performance: It reduces the number of API requests and optimizes data fetching.
- Better user experience: It provides smooth loading states and handles errors gracefully.

Example:

JavaScript

```
import { useQuery } from 'react-query';
```

```
function MyComponent() {

    const { isLoading, error, data } =
useQuery('users', () =>

        fetch('/api/users').then(res =>
res.json())

    );


    if (isLoading) return <div>Loading...</div>;


    if (error) return <div>An error occurred:
{error.message}</div>;


    return (

        <ul>

            {data.map(user => (

                <li
key={user.id}>{user.name}</li>

            ))}

        </ul>

    );

}
```

- useQuery('users', ...): This hook fetches data and caches it under the key 'users'.
- isLoading, error, and data: These variables provide information about the fetching state.

formik and react-hook-form

formik and react-hook-form are libraries that simplify form handling in React. Forms are a core part of many web applications, and these libraries make it easier to manage form state, validation, and submission.

Why are these libraries helpful?

- Simplified form management: They reduce the amount of boilerplate code you need to write for forms.
- Improved validation: They provide tools for validating form inputs.
- Better performance: react-hook-form is known for its performance optimizations.

Example (using react-hook-form):

JavaScript

```
import { useForm } from 'react-hook-form';



function MyForm() {

    const { register, handleSubmit, formState: {
errors } } = useForm();



    const onSubmit = data => console.log(data);
```

```
      return (

          <form onSubmit={handleSubmit(onSubmit)}>

              <input {...register('firstName', {
required: 'First name is required' })} />

              {errors.firstName &&
<p>{errors.firstName.message}</p>}


              <input {...register('lastName')} />


              <button type="submit">Submit</button>

          </form>

      );

}
```

- useForm(): This hook provides functions and state for managing the form.
- register('firstName', { required: ... }): This registers an input field and sets validation rules.
- handleSubmit(onSubmit): This function handles form submission.
- errors: This object contains any validation errors.

styled-components and emotion

styled-components and emotion are CSS-in-JS libraries. They allow you to write CSS directly within your JavaScript code.[7]

Why are these libraries helpful?

- Component-scoped styles: Styles are tied to specific components, preventing CSS conflicts.
- Dynamic styling: You can easily style components based on props or state.
- Improved maintainability: CSS is co-located with the components that use it.

Example (using styled-components):

```javascript
import styled from 'styled-components';


const MyButton = styled.button`

    background-color: ${props => props.primary ?
'blue' : 'gray'};

    color: white;

    padding: 10px 20px;

    border: none;

    cursor: pointer;

`;


function MyComponent() {

    return (

        <div>
```

```
        <MyButton primary>Primary
Button</MyButton>

        <MyButton>Secondary Button</MyButton>

    </div>

  );

}
```

- styled.button: This creates a styled button component.
- background-color: ${props => ...}: This dynamically sets the background color based on the primary prop.

graphql-request and urql

graphql-request and urql are GraphQL client libraries. GraphQL is a query language for APIs, and these libraries make it easier to fetch data from GraphQL APIs.[8]

Why are these libraries helpful?

- Simplified GraphQL fetching: They handle the details of making GraphQL requests.
- Efficient data fetching: GraphQL allows you to fetch only the data you need.[9]

Example (using graphql-request):

```
JavaScript

import { GraphQLClient, gql } from
'graphql-request';
```

```
const client = new GraphQLClient('/graphql'); //
Your GraphQL API endpoint


const query = gql`

    query {

        users {

            id

            name

        }

    }

`;



async function fetchUsers() {

    const data = await client.request(query);

    console.log(data);

}



fetchUsers();
```

- GraphQLClient('/graphql'): This creates a GraphQL client.
- gql\...``: This uses a template literal to define the GraphQL query.
- client.request(query): This sends the query to the GraphQL API.

next-seo

next-seo is a library that helps you optimize your Next.js applications for search engines (SEO).

Why is this library helpful?

- Simplified SEO: It makes it easier to manage meta tags, structured data, and other SEO-related elements.
- Improved search engine visibility: It helps you create websites that are more easily crawled and indexed by search engines.

Example:

```JavaScript
import { NextSeo } from 'next-seo';


function MyPage() {

    return (

        <>

            <NextSeo

                title="My Page Title"

                description="Description of my
page"


canonical="https://www.example.com/my-page"
            />
```

```
        {/* ... page content ... */}

    </>

  );

}
```

- NextSeo: This component sets meta tags like title, description, and canonical.

framer-motion

framer-motion is a library that provides powerful animation capabilities for React components.

Why is this library helpful?

- Simplified animations: It makes it easier to create smooth and engaging animations.
- Improved user experience: Animations can make your application feel more interactive and responsive.[10]

Example:

```JavaScript
import { motion } from 'framer-motion';


function MyComponent() {

    return (

        <motion.div

            animate={{ x: 100 }}
```

```
        transition={{ duration: 0.5 }}

    >

        Animate me!

    </motion.div>

  );

}
```

- motion.div: This creates a div element that can be animated.
- animate={{ x: 100 }}: This animates the x position of the element to 100 pixels.
- transition={{ duration: 0.5 }}: This sets the duration of the animation to 0.5 seconds.

These are just a few of the many useful libraries and tools available in the Next.js ecosystem. It's worth exploring them to discover how they can help you build better Next.js applications.

11.2 Emerging Trends in Next.js Development

Okay, let's talk about the exciting and ever-evolving landscape of Next.js development. It's important to keep an eye on emerging trends, because Next.js is a framework that's constantly pushing the boundaries of what's possible in web development. Staying up-to-date will help you build more efficient, performant, and modern applications.

Next.js is not static; it's a dynamic and living project. The Next.js team and the community are continuously working to improve the framework, add new features, and address the challenges of modern web development.

Here are some of the key trends that are shaping the future of Next.js:

Server Components

Server Components are a groundbreaking feature in React that's poised to have a significant impact on how we build Next.js applications.

What are Server Components?

Normally, in a React application, all your components are rendered on the client-side (in the user's browser). This means that the browser has to download, parse, and execute the JavaScript code for all your components. This can impact performance, especially for complex applications.

Server Components allow you to render certain components on the server. The server renders the component and sends only the resulting UI (the HTML) to the client. The client doesn't have to download or execute the JavaScript code for those components.

Benefits of Server Components:

- Reduced JavaScript Bundle Size: This is the biggest win. By rendering components on the server, you send less JavaScript to the browser, leading to faster initial page loads and improved performance.
- Improved Performance: Less JavaScript to download and execute means faster rendering and a more responsive user experience.
- Data Fetching Optimization: Server Components can directly access server-side resources like databases without needing to create API routes. This can simplify data fetching and improve efficiency.
- SEO Improvements: Server-rendered content is readily available for search engine crawlers, which can improve your website's SEO.

Example (Conceptual):

It's important to note that Server Components have specific rules and are still evolving, so this is a simplified conceptual example to illustrate the core idea:

JavaScript

```
// This component runs ONLY on the server

// It cannot use useState, useEffect, or other
React hooks

// It can directly access the database

server component MyDatabaseComponent() {

    const data = await db.query('SELECT * FROM
my_table');

    return (

        <ul>

            {data.map(item => <li
key={item.id}>{item.name}</li>)}

        </ul>

    );

}


// This is a regular client component

import React, { useState } from 'react';
```

```
function MyClientComponent() {

    const [count, setCount] = useState(0);

    return (

        <div>

            <p>Count: {count}</p>

            <button onClick={() => setCount(count
+ 1)}>Increment</button>

        </div>

    );

}


function MyPage() {

    return (

        <div>

            <h1>My Page</h1>

            <MyDatabaseComponent /> // Server
Component

            <MyClientComponent />    // Client
Component

        </div>

    );

}
```

```
export default MyPage;
```

MyDatabaseComponent is a Server Component. It fetches data directly from the database (this is a simplified representation; you'll still need proper database connection management). Importantly, its JavaScript code is *not* sent to the browser.

MyClientComponent is a regular client component. It uses useState and its JavaScript code *is* sent to the browser.

Key Points about Server Components:

- They have limitations. They cannot use React hooks like useState, useEffect, or browser APIs.
- They are designed for data fetching, rendering content, and tasks that don't require interactivity.
- They can be combined with client components in the same component tree.

Server Components are a major shift in how we build React applications, and they have the potential to significantly improve the performance of Next.js applications.

Middleware

Middleware in Next.js allows you to run code before a request is completed. This is a powerful feature for handling tasks that need to be performed for multiple routes.

What is Middleware?

Think of middleware as a gatekeeper. It sits between the user's request and your Next.js application's route handlers. It can inspect the request, modify it, redirect the user, or even prevent the request from reaching the route handler.

Use Cases for Middleware:

- Authentication and Authorization: Check if a user is authenticated before allowing them to access a protected route.
- Redirects and Rewrites: Redirect users based on their location, device, or other criteria.
- Feature Flags: Enable or disable features based on user groups or other conditions.
- Logging: Log information about incoming requests.
- Internationalization (i18n): Determine the user's preferred language and redirect them to the appropriate version of the site.

Example:

JavaScript

```
// middleware.js


import { NextResponse } from 'next/server';


export function middleware(req) {

    // Check if the user is authenticated
(replace with your actual auth logic)

    const token = req.cookies.get('token');


    if (!token &&
req.nextUrl.pathname.startsWith('/dashboard')) {
```

```
    // Redirect to login page if not
authenticated

        return NextResponse.redirect(new
URL('/login', req.url));

    }


    // Allow the request to continue

    return NextResponse.next();

}


// Configuration (optional)

export const config = {

    matcher: ['/dashboard/:path*'],

};
```

- This middleware checks for a token cookie.
- If the token is missing and the user is trying to access a page under /dashboard, it redirects them to the /login page.
- config.matcher specifies which paths the middleware should run for.

Key Points about Middleware:

- Middleware runs before any route handlers.
- You can access the request and response objects in middleware.
- Middleware can modify the request or response.
- Middleware can redirect or rewrite URLs.

Middleware is becoming increasingly important for building robust and flexible Next.js applications.

Edge Functions

Edge Functions allow you to run server-side code closer to the user. This is a significant performance optimization technique.

What are Edge Functions?

Traditionally, your server-side code runs in a central server. When a user requests a page, the request has to travel to that server, the server processes it, and the response travels back to the user. This distance adds latency, which slows down the response.

Edge Functions, on the other hand, run on edge servers that are distributed globally. This means your code runs closer to the user, reducing latency and improving response times.

Use Cases for Edge Functions:

- Personalization: Tailor content based on the user's location, device, or other factors.
- Authentication: Verify user credentials quickly and efficiently.
- A/B Testing: Split traffic between different versions of your application.
- Redirects and Rewrites: Perform redirects or rewrites based on user agents or other conditions.
- Bot Detection: Identify and block malicious bots.

Example:

```
JavaScript


// middleware.ts (Using TypeScript for better
type safety is common with Edge Functions)
```

```javascript
import { NextResponse } from 'next/server';

import { geoIP } from '@vercel/edge'; // Example:
Using Vercel's geoIP library


export async function middleware(req) {

    const country = geoIP.country(req);


    if (country?.code === 'US') {

        // Redirect users from the US to /us

        return NextResponse.redirect(new
URL('/us', req.url));

    }


    return NextResponse.next();

}


export const config = {

    matcher: '/(.*)', // Run for all routes

};
```

This middleware uses Vercel's geoIP library to determine the user's country.

If the user is from the US, it redirects them to /us.

Key Points about Edge Functions:

- They run on edge servers for low latency.
- They are designed for lightweight, fast operations.
- They have limitations on things like file system access.

Edge Functions are a powerful way to improve the performance and responsiveness of Next.js applications.

Improved Tooling

The Next.js team is constantly working to improve the developer experience by providing better tooling.

This includes:

- Enhanced Error Messages: More informative and helpful error messages.
- Improved Debugging Tools: New features and capabilities in Next.js Devtools.
- Better Build Performance: Optimizations to the build process to make it faster.
- More Comprehensive Documentation: Clearer and more detailed documentation.

Accessibility

There's a growing awareness of the importance of building accessible web applications. Next.js is incorporating features and best practices to make it easier to create websites that are usable by everyone, including people with disabilities.

This includes:

- Semantic HTML: Encouraging the use of semantic HTML elements.

- ARIA Attributes: Providing guidance on using ARIA attributes to enhance accessibility.
- Improved Image Optimization: Ensuring that the next/image component promotes accessible image practices (like requiring alt attributes).

By staying informed about these emerging trends, you can future-proof your Next.js skills and build cutting-edge web applications.

11.3 Real-World Use Cases and Case Studies

Okay, let's talk about how Next.js is being used in the real world. It's not just a theoretical framework; it's a powerful tool that's being adopted by a wide range of companies and organizations to build diverse and impactful web applications.[1] Understanding these real-world applications can give you a better sense of Next.js's capabilities and its relevance in the industry.

Next.js has proven to be versatile, suitable for projects ranging from simple marketing sites to complex, data-driven applications.[2] Its strengths in performance, SEO, and developer experience make it a compelling choice for many different use cases.

Here are some of the key areas where Next.js shines:

E-commerce

E-commerce websites have stringent requirements for performance and SEO.[3] They need to load quickly to provide a smooth shopping experience and rank well in search engine results to attract customers.[4] Next.js is well-suited for these needs.

- Product Pages: Next.js allows you to create highly optimized product pages with features like:

- Server-Side Rendering (SSR): Ensures that product information is readily available for search engine crawlers, improving SEO.[5]
- Static Site Generation (SSG): Can be used for product pages that don't change frequently, providing excellent performance.
- Image Optimization: The next/image component helps optimize product images, reducing load times.

Shopping Carts and Checkout Flows

Next.js can handle the complex logic and data management involved in shopping carts and checkout processes.[6]

Dynamic Content

Next.js can efficiently handle dynamic content like product recommendations and personalized offers.[7]

Real-world example:

Many online retailers use Next.js to build their storefronts.[8] This allows them to create fast, engaging, and SEO-friendly websites that drive sales.

Key takeaway

Next.js helps e-commerce sites deliver a fast and seamless shopping experience, which is crucial for conversion rates and customer satisfaction.[9]

News and Media

News websites and media platforms face the challenge of delivering large amounts of content quickly and efficiently. They also need to ensure that their content is easily discoverable by search engines. Next.js is a strong contender for these applications.

Article Pages

Next.js can be used to create article pages with:

- SSR: Ensures that articles are indexed by search engines.[10]
- Fast Loading Times: Improves user engagement and reduces bounce rates.
- Dynamic Updates: Next.js can handle dynamic updates to articles, such as live comments or breaking news.

Content Management Systems (CMS)

Next.js can be integrated with various CMS platforms to fetch and display content.[11]

Video and Multimedia

Next.js can be used to build platforms that deliver video and multimedia content.[12]

Real-world example:

Several online news publications leverage Next.js to deliver their articles and media content.[13] This helps them provide a fast and responsive experience for their readers.

Key takeaway

Next.js helps news and media outlets deliver content efficiently and improve their search engine visibility, which is essential for reaching a wider audience.[14]

Marketing Websites

Marketing websites need to be visually appealing, performant, and easily discoverable by potential customers. Next.js can be used to create these types of websites effectively.[15]

Landing Pages

Next.js allows you to build highly optimized landing pages that load quickly and convert visitors.[16]

Interactive Experiences

Next.js can be used to create interactive elements and animations that engage users.[17]

SEO Optimization

Next.js helps ensure that marketing websites are easily found by search engines.[18]

Real-world example:

Many companies use Next.js to build their corporate websites and marketing campaigns.[19] This allows them to create visually stunning and performant websites that effectively communicate their brand message.

Key takeaway

Next.js helps marketers create engaging and high-performing websites that drive leads and conversions.[20]

Dashboards

Dashboards often display real-time data and provide interactive visualizations.[21] Next.js can be used to build these complex applications.

Data Visualization

Next.js can be integrated with libraries like Chart.js and D3.js to create interactive charts and graphs.[22]

Real-time Updates

Next.js can handle real-time data updates using technologies like WebSockets.[23]

User Authentication

Next.js can be used to build secure dashboards with user authentication and authorization.[24]

Real-world example:

Many companies use Next.js to build internal dashboards for monitoring key metrics and making data-driven decisions.[25]

Key takeaway

Next.js provides the tools to build interactive and data-rich dashboards that provide valuable insights.[26]

SaaS Applications

Software-as-a-Service (SaaS) applications often require a combination of performance, scalability, and security. Next.js can be a good choice for building these types of applications.

User Interfaces

Next.js allows you to create complex and interactive user interfaces.[27]

API Integration

Next.js can be used to integrate with various APIs.[28]

Authentication and Authorization

Next.js can be used to build secure applications with user authentication and authorization.[29]

Real-world example:

Several SaaS companies use Next.js to build their web applications, providing a robust and scalable platform for their users.[30]

Key takeaway

Next.js offers the flexibility and features needed to build complex and feature-rich SaaS applications.[31]

Important Note:

While I've provided examples of common use cases, Next.js is not limited to these areas. Its flexibility and performance make it suitable for a wide range of web development projects.

To further enhance your understanding, I encourage you to explore case studies and examples of companies using Next.js. This will give you valuable insights into how Next.js is being applied in practice and the benefits it provides.

Conclusion

This book has equipped you with a robust understanding of Next.js, taking you from fundamental concepts to advanced techniques for building modern, dynamic, and performant web applications. We've explored the core architecture of Next.js, including its powerful rendering capabilities with Server-Side Rendering (SSR), Static Site Generation (SSG), and Incremental Static Regeneration (ISR). You've gained the skills to master routing and navigation, effectively handle data fetching, and create scalable API routes and serverless functions.

Furthermore, we've addressed crucial aspects of application development, such as state management with the Context API and Redux/Zustand, advanced component patterns and optimization, and securing your applications through authentication and authorization best practices. We emphasized the importance of performance, covering image optimization, asset management, and various techniques to monitor and enhance your application's speed and responsiveness.

Throughout this learning process, we've stressed the importance of testing and debugging, providing you with the knowledge to write reliable code and efficiently troubleshoot any issues that may arise. Finally, we've broadened your perspective by exploring the Next.js ecosystem, popular libraries and tools, emerging trends, and real-world use cases, preparing you to stay at the forefront of Next.js development.

By mastering the concepts and techniques presented in this book, you are now well-prepared to tackle a wide range of web development challenges with Next.js. You possess the skills to build sophisticated, scalable, and user-friendly applications that meet the demands of the modern web. The journey of learning and growth in web development is ongoing, and this book serves as a strong foundation for your continued exploration and mastery of

Next.js. Embrace the challenges, experiment with the tools, and continue to build amazing web experiences.

www.ingramcontent.com/pod-product-compliance
Lightning Source LLC
LaVergne TN
LVHW080113070326
832902LV00015B/2569